Halsingborg

Helsingor

Espergœrde

Humlebœk ① 1

Kokkedal

② 2

Rungsted ③ 3

Vedbœk

DENMARK

Skovshoved

④ 4

Hellerup
Tuborg

⑤ 5

COPENHAGEN

⑥ 6

⑦ 7

Amager

SWEDEN

Ven

Landskrona

N

⑧ 8

Saltholm

MALMÖ

scale

5

10

15 miles

Elvström speaks....

Other Books by PAUL ELVSTRÖM

Guld Til Danmark
Joller og Kapsejladstaktik
Expert Dinghy and Keelboat Racing
Paul Elvström Explains the Yacht Racing Rules

ELVSTRÖM SPEAKS ON YACHT RACING. Copyright © 1969 by Paul Elvström and Richard Creagh-Osborne. First published in Great Britain in 1970 by Nautical Publishing Company. First American edition published 1970 by Quadrangle Books, Inc. All rights reserved, including the right to reproduce this book or portions thereof in any form. For information, address: Quadrangle Books, Inc., 12 East Delaware Place, Chicago 60611. Manufactured in the United States of America.

Library of Congress Catalog Card Number: 70-116075

SBN 8129-0134-7

Elvström speaks on yacht racing

Edited with an introduction by
Richard Creagh-Osborne

One-Design & Offshore
Yachtsman Magazine
Quadrangle Books

Acknowledgements

The endpaper maps and title-page design are by Keith Blount, L.S.I.A.,
Lymington.

The drawings and sketches within the text and the jacket painting are
by R. M. Coombs, Lymington.

Acknowledgements are also made to the following copyright holders
for the use of some of the photographs:

Presshuset, Copenhagen
Peter Juul, Denmark
Nordisk Pressefoto, Copenhagen
A Traverso, Cannes
Ragnvalds Foto, Copenhagen
Frank Zagerino, Florida
Jens Frellsen, Roskilde
D. Patridis, Athens
Mogens Berger, *Ekstrabladet*
K. Hashimoto, Japan

The remaining photographs are either copyright Paul Elvström or
Richard Creagh-Osborne but if any copyright holders have been
inadvertently missed out, apologies are offered.

Thanks are also given to
John Albrechtson of Goteborg and
One-Design and Offshore Yachtsman of Chicago
for permission to reprint an article which first appeared in that
magazine.

Contents————————————

Foreword

I am writing this book because, after having read the other books I did, people have asked me to tell more of my own stories and, at the same time, tell why I won this and that race; then they could read the stories and, at the same time, learn from them. That gave me the idea of reporting on my life; and, when I think back on all the things that have happened, I really feel that my whole life has been a big adventure. That's the reason that I dare to make such a book, because it is not my nature to tell about myself. My first thought was to ask myself if my story would interest other people. I think that this book, with the technical and rule books I have already done, is meant only to help to make yacht racing more interesting and, at the same time, if it can give me profit, then it will be very nice. I think it is everybody's dream to live and to do what he likes doing, both at the same time.

Paul Elvström

November 1969

Introduction————————————

by Richard Creagh-Osborne

I must say that it is no small problem to work with Paul on a project like this. Having helped him with several books and frequently arranged to meet him at his home or at my home for us to do some work together, I have learned, from the experience of many frustrated hours, that one has to use some degree of subterfuge to get his full attention.

Once Paul came to me to do ten days' work on a book, but he was so obsessed at that time with his new *Trapez* single-hander and the forthcoming IYRU Trials that nothing I could do would keep his mind on the chore of reading and writing. I had misguidedly brought one of his prototype boats back to Lymington a few weeks earlier, and had even lost my senses enough to mention that I had been having some small troubles with various parts. In no time at all Paul was on the doorstep, just itching to start fiddling. And fiddle we did for nine and a half days of his ten-day visit. I think we did about four hours' work on the book! It was all great fun, and interesting in its way, but it did not matter in the least to Paul that there were deadlines to be met with printers—he is absolutely single-minded when he has a problem on his mind. It is perhaps even more exasperating that, when a problem is finally solved, he will suddenly announce that he is tired, and just go to sleep!

On other occasions I have been to Denmark and trailed round behind Paul as he dashed from place to place, hoping for a few quiet moments when I could get his undivided attention. The truth is that reading and writing are anathema to Paul. If he can avoid either, he is a happy man and, if he can sidestep both, his day is made. However, talking is his strong suit, and so I finally obtained a small tape recorder and persuaded him to talk and to ignore the machine.

To my surprise Paul took to this method with enthusiasm when we

9

met to try it out during the period of the IYRU Meetings in November 1968; so, striking whilst the iron was hot, so to speak, I picked on the gloomiest and coldest three days I could find in January, judging that Paul would be bored and depressed, and took the 'plane to Copenhagen.

It was fifteen degrees colder in Denmark, with hardly any daylight, and I was rewarded with no fewer than three days of non-stop talk which is now the bones of this book. I have tried to get Paul to talk about every part of his sailing life, but I am sure there are still many facets we have not covered. Nevertheless, I hope that enough emerges to portray this remarkable sailing genius, and to show the sort of qualities which are needed to accomplish such a vast range of success.

On another occasion in the autumn of 1968, I arrived at Copenhagen's Kastrup Airport and was met by the usual smiling, bouncing Paul, who took my brief-case and marched outside.

It was a lovely evening as we emerged on to the car park, and I set off towards the place where he usually parked the Mercedes. But Paul turned to the right and took a bicycle which was leaning in solitary state against the bare expanse of the airport terminal wall. He grabbed my grip, put it and the brief-case on to the carrier, and strode off, pushing the bicycle. I followed, wondering dimly if we were going to have to walk the ten miles to his home at Hellerup.

But Paul would say nothing, whilst thoughts of Elvström Sails going broke, or Paul having been picked up by the police and losing his driving licence, or of some new passion for physical fitness flashed through my mind.

And then, as we went out via the motorway and turned right toward the Sound, I remembered an occasion when I flew into Fornebu Airport at Oslo, (incidentally without a passport, but that's another story), to be met by Harald Eriksen, the then President of the Finn Association, who led me to the end of the airport runway, where his large, fast, open-roofed motor-launch was tied up to a rock. We had climbed aboard, to be greeted by two beautiful Norwegian girls and a splendid table of refreshments. We then picked up two more Finn sailors from other points round the fjord, and so began in splendidly Scandinavian style an International Finn Class Technical Committee Meeting. Thus it is that the very best of class rules are made!

We have digressed somewhat; but I was right this time. Paul led the way to a small yacht harbour outside the airport, where his small *Crescent* speed boat was tied up. He folded the bicycle, we put ourselves and the bags aboard, and we were off at 30 knots.

In no time at all we had whisked up the coast past the big commerical harbour, stopped for a few seconds to give advice to some Navy youngsters sailing a *Trapez* dinghy in the evening race, then zoomed past Tuborg Brewery and the little, tree-fringed Hellerup yacht harbour, to stop finally opposite the familiar house on the sea wall.

This was typical Paul—a passion for boats and boating. He knew also that all his friends would prefer to come by sea to his house, and he often used to use his bigger power catamaran to commute to the sail-loft, when it was situated up the coast at Rungsted.

We laughed about this, but I said to Paul that he ought to advertise by having a fleet of trade bicycles at Kastrup Yacht Harbour with "Elvström Sails" written on them, and to fetch all his most important customers by bicycle and sea.

"...a fleet of trade bicycles..."

I first met Paul only in 1956, when he had already won two Olympic Gold Medals, and was just about to win a third. It was Easter, and the first Finn Gold Cup was being held at Burnham-on-Crouch, in some of the most bitterly cold weather in which I have ever sailed. The sea froze on the decks and the ropes refused to render through blocks, whilst the wind howled constantly down the bleak and wintry Crouch estuary.

The British had made one of their occasional major advances in boat fittings by developing and commercially producing a semi-automatic bailer. All the British boats had the new "Lewmar" tube-bailer and, in these conditions, were at a distinct advantage. After the first two days' racing, Paul and other overseas skippers were to be seen with numbed fingers drilling holes in their boats, and fitting new bailers from a stock thoughtfully provided by one of the more enterprising British *Finn* sailors.

11

The following day, however, was cold but sunny and there was almost no wind. I kept company with Paul for hours, drifting up and down the Crouch way back in the fleet, until we finally decided to race each other back to the club, and thus it was that I scored one of my very few racing successes over the *maestro*. For years afterwards Paul would laugh and pull my leg about my very long paddle that was so fast!

Beaten by a longer paddle!

Paul has no vestige of snobbery in his make-up. He is naturally pleased to have become a personal friend of the Greek Royal Family, but he is interested in them mainly as charming people and for their great interest in yachting. Paul will talk with enthusiasm for hours with King or schoolboy, with world champions or local club beginners; it matters not who they are, as long as they show a real interest in racing.

He is completely honest and genuine. Deviousness and even gamesmanship do not come easy to him should it ever occur to him to use such tactics. This can be disconcerting to those who go to him for advice and it has been not unknown for sailors to complain that they have been purposely misled to their cost, when the exact opposite was the intention.

It happens because Paul's mind races ahead continually as he picks new ideas from the air and from discussions, which then prompt him to make some new experiment in sail shape or boat-handling techniques. Thus, his honest opinion one week might be completely altered or even reversed a week later, to the consternation of those who have made a pilgrimage to hear words from the oracle.

Nevertheless, the fact is that, if you ask him a question, you will

Paul talks to King Constantine at the Copenhagen Boat Show.

Presshuset

get a complete and honest answer on the situation as it seems to him at that moment. Thus Paul's story of how he replied to a Press query before the 1952 Helsinki Olympics by saying that he was sure he would win the Gold Medal was an absolutely honest assessment. The Press and the public were shocked at his apparently big-headed boasting, but Paul did nothing less than answer the question with the truth, and was genuinely surprised by the reaction. This näiveté is characteristic, especially when he has warmed up to his subject in a discussion.

Paul has changed considerably since his nervous breakdown in 1960. Previous to this, his determination and single-mindedness were absolute when it came to business or racing and, in turn, tuning and racing a boat were the subjects which occupied his whole life and thoughts. His friends were solely racing yachtsmen, and his conversa-

... will talk with enthusiasm for hours ...

tion was only on yacht racing and allied subjects. He loved and needed his charming wife, Anne, and his home and family, whilst at the same time, in day to day matters, his yacht racing always came first. He would never have abandoned his home life had it ever become a matter of deciding on one or the other, but he knew at the back of his mind that he had to do this thing and that, in the long term, it would benefit the family. Anne was wise enough to let him do it.

Paul says now that he realizes it must have been hard for Anne in those early days, but when a man and wife are both young, they are determined to make something tangible of their life together and are prepared to sacrifice a great deal to achieve this. Anne most certainly played a vital part in Paul's success and, now that his philosophy of life has changed so much, she is able to reap a reward from the sacrifices she made in the hard times of the racing years.

In the last chapter of this book Paul reveals something of his present views on life and sailing. Any of us who read this life story and who have had even a small spark of ambition to achieve success will see here magnified all the problems which face us in attempting to reach our goal.

Paul started by wanting to be the best in sailing. Later, after having proved himself the best with two Gold Medals behind him, he revealed to his brother that his aim was to win six Gold Medals. He now confesses that he could never have done this. His burning ambition had reached its peak with the 1960 Olympic races and, apart from a World Championship in 1962 as crew in a *Flying Dutchman,* he did not race again for three years.

Paul's nervous energy had driven him on toward peaks never before attempted by any other sailor. His story shows the lengths to which he had to go to achieve such success; but eventually there came a point where the physical body could take no more, and he was forced to stop. He only just succeeded in completing the 1960 Olympic series, and did not start in the last race through physical illness, which was a symptom of this final stress.

Paul tells of the years he spent watching races, and how he eventually came to terms with himself so that he could take up racing again without wearing himself out. The final turning point was the 1964 Olympic Games, which he watched from a spectator boat. He finally realized how silly it was to make such an intense fight of something which should be only a pleasure. So then followed four years of

Paul spent the "waiting years" photographing boats and watching races. Here in Tokyo in 1964 he contemplates his return to the sport.

racing for sheer fun and nothing else. His business was a success, thanks to his diligence during the three "watching" years and, for the first time, he was able to indulge himself in the real pleasure of racing.

But for his competitors there was really no relief. Paul's experience was unmatched and his expertise was, if anything, improved by his years of watching races. In 1966 he demonstrated this as the result of a challenge and a friendly bet, by winning two major World Championships and being a very close runner-up in a third, all in the space of one year.

However, in spite of Paul's great store of experience and his profound technical knowledge, he is the first to admit that a vital spark has gone out of his racing. He no longer takes the immense trouble

In 1968 at Acapulco Paul has completely regained his usual boisterous spirits.

necessary to be certain of the best start—considered by him to be the most taxing and essential part of winning a yacht race. He is still a formidable competitor but now, if he feels he is not going to enjoy himself, he simply will not take part. He likes racing only in classes where the atmosphere and spirit match his own, and he often decides to stay at home and take his eldest girls water ski-ing or winter-sporting to the Alps, rather than go out of his way to win some championship.

In the early days Paul was very poor in light winds. He was impatient in conditions where he could not use his great strength to advantage; but, though a big and powerful man, he is a true athlete, and his balance and dexterity are superlatively good.

Once Pierre Poullain and I were struggling to get my *Finn* up a slip, and making little progress however hard we pulled and lifted. Paul appeared, and waved us aside. He grabbed the stemhead handle with one hand and, with a mighty lunge, the boat was at the top. Another time a party of us went to the famous amusement park of Bakken near his home, and were trying to knock down targets with rifles. We were having little success until Paul appeared, took a rifle and scored direct hits with every shot. He had never done this before, and no-one was more surprised than he was.

There is no doubt that his strength was a major factor in his success in the *Finn* class. Before the days of soft rigs, cam cleats, bailers and winch blocks, the *Finn* was a brutish boat in winds above force three, but Paul was able to play his sheet whilst sailing to windward through waves, whilst the rest of us were struggling merely to hold the sheet at all. As he says in his story, in medium and strong winds he had no competition in this class.

If Paul has a failing, it is in a stubbornness and an inability to accept advice in any form directly. It is untrue to say that he will never accept advice, because his friends will frequently have noticed how suggestions made and brusquely rejected have been taken up, perhaps weeks, months or even years later, though the original source has seldom been acknowledged. He has to work out the problem in his own way and in his own time.

This attitude has been costly for Paul, both in time and money. Some of his business ideas and inventions could never have worked, but no amount of hinting from friends could deter him until it had become so painfully obvious that even he could not fail to see it. Perhaps the saddest example from my point of view, and certainly the most costly from Paul's, was his *Trapez* class dinghy.

Paul spent two years developing that boat as a single-hander before taking it to the IYRU Trials at Weymouth. He made at least two complete sets of fibre-glass moulds and spent an enormous amount of

17

time and money, almost to no avail at all. The overall concept was exciting and entirely novel: one ultra-modern hull, absolutely one-design even to the fittings, and with four rigs using two different masts to make four separate classes of boat.

It was intended that his one factory should produce everything and that all the parts and the sails should be exactly similar. The idea was that a series of first-class racing boats should be made at an absolutely rock-bottom price, on account of standardization and quantity production. The guarantee of its success would be that the boat was conceived and presented by Elvström—nothing more and nothing less. International racing would be encouraged, because the hulls need not be transported, and a competitor had to carry only the sails which were

From the left: Paul's daughters Trine, Gitte, Stine and Pia with Paul on the ski slopes.

the sole part personal to each skipper. Indeed, it was intended that every sail should have its own individual sail number put on in the factory before make-up—another great saving in cost—so that the purchase of a new sail meant a new number also.

To save unnecessary expense for competitors, they could enter a regatta under only one sail number, and hence only one sail could be used in any one series. The only item that need be measured at any regatta was the sail. It would immediately be obvious, from a purely cursory inspection, if any non-standard fitting was being used on the boat. Sails were to be sewn with special coloured thread to discourage alterations to the cut.

There was to be a big organization with spares and service

18

departments world-wide, based initially on the existing loose association of Elvström agents, whilst national organizers would control the class and rule on disputes and complaints.

The whole grand concept was ambitious and could just have succeeded if it had been launched at that particular time when the IYRU was searching for a one-man, and later a two-man, international boat. Charges of monopoly and so on would undoubtedly have arisen and the IYRU themselves would not, at that time, have been sufficiently advanced in their thinking to have been able to associate themselves with so commercially organized a project. Nevertheless, it could have caught the public imagination at that time and, if it had succeeded,

The simple and utterly modern moulding of the prototype Trapez *class dinghy.*

Paul would certainly have been co-operative in handing it over later to the IYRU.

The whole thing failed, ironically because Paul could not bring himself to have someone else actually design the boat. Thus the hull shape was not right, and the details of the construction and rig had faults which, in spite of so long a period of development, were not satisfactory by the time of the IYRU trials.

Paul later altered the hull shape and modified the other matters and now the class is expanding rapidly in Scandinavia, but the original grand concept has been lost irretrievably. The world-wide universal family of one-design boats which could conceivably have been in everybody's backyard today will now never come to pass, because only

19

Trapez *class dinghies racing single-handed off Denmark.*

a genius such as Paul Elvström could have engineered the enthusiasm and goodwill which would have been needed to get such a project off the ground. It could have been done only by a brilliant "dictator"; but, like all such spirits, they suffer from some shortcoming which in the end proves fatal to their great ideals.

There is no doubt that Paul Elvström is a practical genius at yacht racing. There are others who are as good at racing as he in a particular class or area, but no-one has been so universally successful in such a wide range of classes and in all parts of the world. We are fortunate also that he is such a colourful and extrovert character, and one who has used his energies to advance the sport so much. The influence of his tuning and sailmaking methods have spread so that racing boats everywhere are both easier and safer to sail, as well as being faster.

This is not the last that we shall hear of Paul Elvström; but I am proud of being in the position of being able to record at this stage of his sailing life his own words on his career and the lessons he has learnt, as well as some practical advice for all his fellow competitors, to help them in handling and racing their boats today.

One————————————————

Early life and racing

Paul Bert Elvström was born on the 25th February, 1928 in the house on the sea wall overlooking the Sound between Denmark and Sweden, where he still lives today. This house is important in this story, not only because its very situation and convenience enabled Paul to develop his talents unhindered by delays of distance and time, but because the lower two floors became the first Elvström sail loft. Besides this, nearly all Paul's international sailing friends first met him when they knocked on his door, in search of one of his early *Finn, Snipe, Pirat* or *Dragon* sails for their boats.

Paul's father was a sea captain, but he died whilst Paul was still young, and his mother was left alone to bring up Paul and his elder brother and younger sister. There was also an older brother who was drowned at the age of five, when he fell into the water off the sea wall. Paul's mother brought up the family quite strictly, but Paul always seems to have had very different capabilities from those of his brother who is now a successful ear, nose and throat surgeon, and his sister who is a dentist. Paul feels he had a great handicap. He put it this way:

Paul. I am word blind. I can't read and I can't write. I get a headache and then I can't think. In school I was the worst in the class. I was not lazy, but I just couldn't read. It was such a big handicap for me.

So maybe I had to try and express myself in another way. I only say "maybe" because I am not sure, but I loved being on the water and just to sit in a rowing dinghy in the evening and look at the water was a dream. But I had the spirit of fighting and, because I liked to be on the water then, I wanted to be the best in water sport. It must be something inside me, because in football, in running, in skating, in ski-ing and everything I want to be the best.

Certainly Paul had many incentives to take up a life connected with the sport of sailing. His home is a roomy villa at the end of a cul-de-sac off the main road leading north out of Copenhagen. It is a few minutes' walk from the centre of Hellerup, the last suburb of Copenhagen, before the road breaks out onto the charming beech-fringed coast with its string of small places, each with its own small harbour and leading up to the narrow ferry crossing to Sweden at Helsingor, (Elsinore).

The famous Tuborg brewery dominates the southern end of Hellerup, with its tall chimneys visible for miles and, at night, the huge

The house on the sea wall, when it was being used as a sail loft and showing the rickety staging before this was swept away by the ice.

23

neon sign acting as a useful guide for becalmed evening sailors on their slow homeward drift to tiny, tree-lined Hellerup yacht harbour.

A little further south is the huge Copenhagen Yacht Marina, situated just inside the moles of the commercial harbour, whilst a mile or so to the north of Hellerup is the fine yacht haven of Skovshoved, which supports splendid fleets of racing keelboats, off-shore cruiser-racers and hundreds of dinghies.

A few yards from the front windows of the house is the sea wall, with the nearly fresh Baltic water lapping at its foot. One can wade out a hundred yards or so on a sandy bottom until one reaches the small power boat that Paul keeps off-lying and uses just as you or I would the family shopping car. A little further out, but still within a hundred yards of the wall, is a deeper water mooring for the *Knaarboat* or *Soling*, or whatever keelboat happens to be being raced or tested at that time.

When I first knew Paul he had a wooden slip off the top of the wall, and a rickety cat-walk leading out to two equally unsteady stagings on which were mounted the test rigs for his sail loft. All this was swept away in the great freeze-up of 1963, and has only recently been replaced by a well-engineered pier terminating in an exceedingly buoyant and frolicsome large floating pontoon. The tidal range is almost nil here, and so Paul likes to have a platform low enough to be able to haul up dinghies or attend to a power boat propeller.

Early racing

Paul. I started sailing because I was born by the water and could watch the races, and I became enthusiastic about it and wanted to race myself. I remember once that my brother was racing in a dinghy against two others. It was a rowing dinghy with a sail, and I had the feeling that I would like to do it myself.

I started playing tennis when I was ten and then football as well when I was eleven. At the same time I became a member of Hellerup Sailing Club—the Junior Club—but they had no dinghies, only keelboats. The boat I sailed was the *Juniorboat,* a little clinker keelboat looking like a miniature *Folkboat,* and we were three in the crew.

The club had thirteen *Juniorboats* and at the start I was crewing. Even then it did not interest me very much to crew, because I had the feeling all the time I could keep the tiller better than the helmsman.

In those days if I was not in the school the teacher knew that I was sailing, and I was very bad in the school. The only interest I had was sailing fast, and when the Hellerup Sailing Club had a summer cruise of fourteen days and we sailed from place to place, I was always racing.

24

Paul, in the middle, is obviously an extrovert even at this age.

Early racing

I wanted to be the first always under all conditions. Even if I had bad luck with the wind I wanted to be first. It was something inside me, and I think this gave me a lot of experience.

Even when I was thirteen years old, if I should take part in a race, I was so well prepared that I had the feeling that I could not lose. The bottom of my boat was always the nicest and every small detail on the whole boat was strong and was exactly perfect, so that I was sure that I had the best boat, the best tuning and the best gear. I only had to start and not make any big mistakes. I had a club boat and I remember the rules were not very strict and I had two old sails, both cotton, and new boats from our club had bigger sails—really bigger in area—but the control was very weak, so in light wind I had absolutely no chance against them. But when the wind came, we were sure winners. But the bottom was the nicest and everything that I could do to the boat was absolutely better than the others. I was really prepared to win.

25

When I was thirteen, my neighbour bought an *Oslo-dinghy*. He said he bought it because he wanted me to teach him to sail. He was a man of forty or so. I asked if I might use it for racing because, at that time, there were about twelve *Oslo-dinghies* in the Sound, and he said, "Of course. Yes." I later realized he did not really want to learn sailing. It did not interest him very much, but he liked me and he thought that I should have a boat and my mother hadn't much money to buy one. So I borrowed the boat and I sailed it nearly every day, and kept it as my own.

Soon after I first got the *Oslo-dinghy* I sailed with a friend along the coast, and outside Vedbaek harbour (see map on front end paper) were five *Oslo-dinghies* racing. We went to the harbour to buy an ice-cake and on the way back they came in and were about to start again. So then we asked if we could join in. This chap who said "yes" told me the story later. He said, "I remember as clearly as if it was today that a little chap with fair hair came holding an ice-cake and asked if he could join the race. We said, "Yes, of course", because he would not disturb anything. Then the small boy started last, but he passed us and continued and when he was at the finishing line we were very far away so that we could hardly see him. Then he disappeared along the coast towards Hellerup, and we never saw him again until we met him later in the annual race at Skovshoved, (see map). We did not know who it was or anything. He just appeared, beat us all and disappeared. We were fifteen years older and we felt very stupid."

In the first official race I took part in off Skovshoved, there were about twelve *Oslo-dinghies*. I was thirteen years and there was only this one race in the year. So that's the reason that all the boats in the Sound were there. I came second after Niels Benzon, who is now the President of the Royal Danish Yacht Club, and I know why. The *Oslo-dinghy* in those days had a sail which had a gaff passing the mast (*a dipping lug*), and so you had to pass the gaff from side to side when you tacked and I didn't know that. Also I had a strap from the lowest part of the gaff to the mast, to make the sail a little fuller near the gaff. Because of that strap I couldn't dip the gaff. It was the first time I had met another *Oslo-dinghy* and I saw the others were moving the gaff from side to side. So on the next run I cut that strap to be able to dip the gaff and after that I came closer and closer to the leading boat, but I didn't catch him, so I came second.

This little story shows how already Paul was obsessed by the drive for success in competition. There are not many sailors of Paul's age who can recall instances of such perception in yacht racing at such an early age. Even today, when dinghy racing is many hundreds of times more popular and there are thousands of children racing boats in large and keen fleets, it would be unusual to find someone not only already so dedicated, but also capable of working out an improvement in tuning and then, at short notice, realizing that there was something even more important that had been forgotten and to have corrected it on the spot.

His competitors over the years will recognize this absolute ruthlessness with his boats. It does not matter what happens to the boat so long as it can be made to carry him to the finishing line first. Cut this—move that—take away the other—Paul had no feeling in him for a boat as a beautiful thing.

We had returned one day from a race in the 1959 Finn Gold Cup, and were on the slip outside his house. Something was wrong with the rudder pintle, and Paul wanted to get at the nuts inside the aft buoyancy tank. He jumped into the boat and, with one mighty kick, the tank panel

27

was a splintered mass of chippings.

This boat, his old Borresen-built *Finn,* similar to the ones made for the 1952 Olympic Games at Helsinki, was the only boat I can recall belonging to him to which he actually gave a name—*Bes.* The *Star, Scandale,* with which he won the World Championship twice, was bought at the last minute from his Swedish friend John Albrechtson, and came complete with its previous name.

The others had no names—just their registered numbers. To Paul they were just tools to be used and, like tools, they had to be ground and sharpened and honed, so that they were perfect for their purpose. As for painting or decorating a boat to beautify it, such a thing would not have occurred to him.

So Paul Elvström's official racing career started with a race for *Oslo-dinghies* on the Sound. We shall shortly see how he developed to become a legend in his own lifetime. Now, at the age of forty-two, he can look back on a string of successes, any one of which would have satisfied most of us. National, Nordic, European and other "local" championships were won at various times, but only considered by Paul as stepping stones to the ultimate goal.

Paul won his first Olympic Gold Medal at the age of twenty, not in itself a record but, owing to the war, it was, of course, not possible for him to have entered a previous competition. As is well known, he then went on to win three more Gold Medals in succession. At the same time he has won World Championships in the *Finn, 5-0-5, Flying Dutchman, Snipe, Star, 5·5-metre* and *Soling* classes. This then is the bare bones of a unique racing career. But how exactly did he do it?

At the end of the war there was almost no dinghy racing in Denmark. There were a few *Oslo-dinghies* and also a fleet of about thirty boats of the British *12-ft. National* dinghy class, which were built on account of the enthusiasm of a British bridge engineer who was working in the country. These boats came in useful later, as shall be seen.

Paul now continues with his story of his early racing days:

Wartime racing
W-boats

Paul. The next boat I sailed was a *W-boat* (pronounced Vee-boat). It is a nice boat, faster than a *Dragon* and there is a story I would like to tell here and it is about a man who still lives today. He owned a *W-boat* and every Saturday afternoon there was a race outside the Little Mermaid at Langelinie. (See map on end paper). We started there and then out into Copenhagen Harbour, outside the harbour and then back. It was during the war and must have been in 1942. A Junior asked

28

me if I could crew instead of him in the *W-boat*. I said, "yes", and he asked me if I had set the spinnaker before. I said, "oh yes", but I had never sailed with a spinnaker; however, I had seen one and I had thought that there would not be any problem. I went to the chap who was steering the boat, who was not the owner. He said to me, "What do you want?" I said that I was to crew instead of the other boy. He said, "You? I am sure that if you held on to the sheets they would take you out with them through the blocks." I became angry and said, "I will show him that I will not pass through the blocks!" Then the third crew member did not come, and we were only us two.

We were six boats and we beat out through Copenhagen Harbour and arrived third at the first mark. Then he said, "Have you set the spinnaker before?", and I said "No", and so he said, "O.K., take the

"... my neighbour bought an Oslo-*dinghy".*

tiller". So I took it. The first boat was steered by the later Bronze Medal winner at Torquay in *Dragons*, Willy Berntsen. He sailed perfectly, put up the spinnaker and so on. The second boat's skipper was busy with his spinnaker, so I took the chance and luffed up and took his wind and then our spinnaker was set O.K., and so we passed him. The other chap in my boat said, "Gosh! Maybe you should keep the tiller all the time." But he took it back, and finished second, but we nearly won because we closed with the leader. That was fun!

I never sailed again in the *W-boat*, because I then became a crew in a *Dragon*. I crewed a lot for Henning Jensen, who later won the Gold Cup in *Dragons* at Medemblik in Holland.

I remember once we were talking about sailing, and I had seen a race he won. He came too late to the start, and the leading group went into no wind, and so he went to the shore and got the wind and won. He won a big cup, and then I said to him, "Oh! You were lucky!" He became so angry and said, "lucky?", so I quickly said, "Oh, excuse me. I meant that you were lucky that there was such a big cup for that race." So then he couldn't say any more. But that taught me something that it is never nice to say that anyone is lucky to win a race, because you are only lucky if you do something you can't foresee. That's luck. But you could not say that he couldn't see that there was wind coming along the shore, and if he had he would have been stupid to have continued and followed the others.

You can say someone has bad luck to lose a race. No-one will argue against that, but already at that stage it taught me what is luck and what is not luck. But it made it all right with Henning by saying that he was lucky that there was such a big cup. I never forgot that.

So I continued crewing a lot in *Dragons,* because they had the best competition. On Saturdays and Sundays we were in a fleet of about fifty *Dragons* in the Sound. It was absolutely the best class.

In 1943 we were not allowed to sail in the Sound any more, so we moved the *Junior-boats* to a lake near Copenhagen, three-quarters of an hour away by bicycle, and I went there every night—absolutely every evening. On Saturdays and Sundays we took our bicycles and we had five boats at another place, at Ise Fjord, and it took us one hour and a quarter to go there. So it was hard work to get out sailing; but for us, when we have the water just outside our house, it was awful to have to go so far. And what was annoying was to sail on a lake where you get this brown, dirty water in your mouth and you look forward to get salt water on your face again. All the *Dragons* went to another place, and so I was only able to sail *Junior-boats*. In '43 I became helmsman in

30

the *Junior-boat* when I won my white anchor badge, and then I was sailing *Junior-boats* all the time.

From that time I won the championship in Hellerup Sailing Club three times. I competed three times and won each time. This is the most difficult thing to win as a junior. At that time Hellerup Sailing Club had all the best helmsmen, and when we had club team races we always won. In most open regattas we changed boats and, never mind what boat I got, I could win. But that was on the local place here in Copenhagen, and so from that time I knew I was a better skipper than the others who were racing here and, as a crew before I got my helmsman's badge, it was very interesting for me to sail with older boys, because they couldn't keep the tiller as I would like the tiller kept. And what's more, in the old days in *Junior-boats,* most helmsmen were sitting in the leeside of their boats even in good strong winds. I was one of the first who got the crew hanging out and, in those days, they didn't understand the position of the weight, and I *can't* understand why, but it was like that. I think I must have had a feeling for balance always.

A Junior-boat *of the Hellerup Sailing Club.*

31

The family *Dragon*   So, after the war, my brother bought a *Dragon* and I wanted to compete in the selection trials for the Torquay Olympic Games in the *Dragon* class. But the boat we had was so slow that we never got the boat ready, but even if we had done so, we could never have won. The boat was made of larch and was basically so slow and the mast was so heavy and the sails that we had were hopeless. We could not pull in the mainsheet as hard as we wanted because the mainsail would tear. It was cotton from the wartime period.

At that time there was import restriction and we could not buy new sails. But other *Dragon* sailors got Ratsey sails by going via Sweden or something like that, but we had no experience of how to do this. So I got my first real genoa when I went to the Olympics in '48 and got a sail from Ratsey. When I came home I won the first race with the new genoa. This sail made the whole difference.

I sailed *Dragons* I think for about seven years, first as crew and then as helmsman. My brother and I shared the boat, but my problem was in every race where I made a good start and good tactics, when we came to a close reach or a beam reach without spinnaker we couldn't do anything. The lighter, mahogany boats all passed us, and I used to say that I would look forward to the day when I would go back to a dinghy where I don't have to fight against money.

But I learned a lot sailing against people who could buy everything, and today I have not forgotten this experience. That's the reason I like to make boats that everybody can afford to buy, and get fair competition such as in my *Trapez* class where you are not allowed to have any advantage on account of your having more money.

Two —————————————————————————

The first two gold medals

You have to practise all the time if you are to be the best. For instance, if you stop sailing races in the winter-time, you will find you have forgotten a lot when you start again in spring-time, and that's what I found when preparing for racing in the *Finn* class. But I think that before I speak about training and tuning I should talk about the Olympics in '48.

I *really* worked hard to go to England, and did all that I could to win. For instance, I had never before sailed in a British *12-ft National* dinghy, which was the type of boat used for the selection trials in Denmark, and I had never been in anything like this boat before. It was the nearest type that we could get to the *Firefly,* which was to be the Olympic boat.

I was selected from my club as a good *Junior-boat* and *Dragon* sailor. When I went to Hellerup Sailing Club to draw for a boat before the first race, I had my clothes and everything ready, and so I went out on to the water one hour before the others. It was a good, strong wind and I tacked and tacked, and then I was reaching and running. So after that hour I said, "Now I will win, because I know the boat." We started and I was lucky that this boat I took was a good one, and I moved away from the fleet and won easily. But I didn't know then that my boat was a good one, so I said to myself, "Now I hope that my boat was not too good, and let us see." Then I won the next two races, too, even though I had bad boats.

O.K., everything went fine and I won the trials, but why I tell you this is to show that, even before the first race in the selection trials, I prepared as much as I could. I did *everything* that I could do to win.

We had no *Fireflies.* We couldn't get permission of the government

to import any, and so the first time I saw a *Firefly* was when I got to
Torquay. As far as I remember, I did not borrow a *12-ft National* in
Denmark, because the people who were the owners of these boats did
not offer to lend them and, at the same time, I was shy of asking.
People would laugh at you at that time if you would prepare in a way
so that you had a better chance to win. In those days, practising for
something just wasn't thought to be the right thing to do.

Just before the final race I capsized and the Selection Committee
said, "How can you ask to go to the Olympics when you can't keep the
boat upright?" I tell you that before I finally won the selection it was a
hard fight with three people, and they continued and continued until
the Committee was sure who was the best. I became better and better
and in the last race I had the worst boat and still I won, and then they
said, "O.K. Finish!" But even then they could not believe that a *Dragon*
sailor could win. It must have taken three weeks of solid racing.

Then I saw a picture of a *Firefly* during the selection trials, and I
realized that if you wanted to tack fast you must cleat your mainsail
and only have to change the jib sheet. I found out later this was the
opposite to what they were doing in England. They were cleating the
jib automatically and holding the main sheet, but I had never seen
anything and so I worked it out in a way so that, before I tacked, I

eased the main sheet just a little, so that it only helped to gain speed.
So I was not pointing just before the tack. Then I tacked and the main
was not sheeted in too hard, so it was safe and it was fast. Otherwise I
might have been hit by a wave and the boat would stop completely and
maybe capsize. That was really a keelboat idea, because when you tack
a keelboat, you free the sheet slightly and then pull it in when you get the
speed again.

To be able to do this, I had to have a cleat I could move from side
to side and in those days such a fitting didn't exist. But I made it, and
so I had it in my suitcase on my way to England, and I asked for
permission to put it in and I got the permission. I did not know what we
were going to be allowed to do to the boats beforehand, and so I had
to make this cleat even though it might never have been used. I made
nothing else except the cleat, because I found that it was enough to be
able to tack fast. That's all.

Before I went to England I asked my employer for one free week
to sail eight hours a day and put this cleat on a *12-ft National,* so that I
could become used to it. Again, you can see, I was prepared. But in those
eight days I realized that I was not strong enough to hang out properly,
but I couldn't get the physical training in eight days. Impossible!

34

When I came to Torquay I was shy and I didn't come out in time
for the first practice race because I didn't know there was one. So I
joined in at the middle of the fleet, and I had the feeling that I
couldn't do anything in speed. And then we came to the first race and,
soon after the start, I had to tack for Palmgreen of Finland. He was on
starboard and he was three boat lengths from me. He had no chance to
hit me or anything, but I was so shy that I left the course. I didn't want to
get into trouble and so I retired from that first race. I was in the middle of
the fleet at the time, but it would have been, of course, important to
get some experience in that race.

Before I left Denmark, everybody said, "If you will not be the last,
we'll be happy", and I felt I couldn't disappoint anyone, and so when I
had to leave the course I was feeling very low inside me. Then I said,
"O.K. you shall not be the last", and in the next race I came sixth, and
my speed was good, and I started feeling the boat better.

After that it went quite well, and then I realized my complex had
disappeared. I was a little anxious in the stronger wind against
Rickard Sarby of Sweden and Koos de Jongh of Holland because they
had the weight and they were really keeping their boats upright. Then
after the fifth race I worked out that if I should have *any* chance at all
for a good place at the end, I should have to win the last two races.

I remember the race before the last I started at the starboard end
of the line. I was pointing much better than the rest of the fleet but the
wind headed and so I tacked. At the start I had *nearly* the direction to
the mark and afterwards when the wind headed—it was very shifty
wind that day—I tacked and I had nearly the direction to the mark on
the other tack. Everyone was pointing towards my transom instead of
tacking. We had four or five more tacks and all the time I had the

Rickard Sarby, the designer of the Finn *and an
Olympic Bronze Medallist.*

35

direction closest to the mark and so I came to the first mark I think about a minute before the second boat.

It was a medium wind and so after that I sailed carefully. I mean that I thought that I sailed carefully because I was not clever enough then to know that in a shifty wind you must only sail to follow the wind and not cover the others. Because I covered them I lost it all but at that time I had thought I was safe. I just won but that was a big lesson which I never forgot.

But then in the last race when I had a chance to win, then my tactic was only to win the race because if this happened and the American was No. 4 or lower then I should win the Gold Medal. He should be No. 3 to win. It was blowing hard and I had never been sailing a *Firefly* or a *12-ft National* in so strong a wind. I was, I think, 72 kilos and de Jongh and Sarby were more than 80 and so I had a complex against them. They went out with full main and full jib and I was *sure* I couldn't do that. So I put four rolls on the mainsail and the full jib. On the way out to the start I realized that I couldn't keep the boat upright, so I lowered the jib and I started with only the small reefed mainsail. And then I hoped the wind would increase. That was the only hope I could have.

I started again by the windward mark and Sarby started at the lee end. He got a good windshift, tacked and passed ahead of me with full main and full jib. I realized that I was slower than Sarby, but I had much better tactics than the others. They were faster but I could also tack faster in the windshifts. So I came second to the first mark, and then downwind de Jongh came past and Herbulot of France also, but when Herbulot should have gybed round the next mark, he continued straight on because he couldn't do anything. Then he luffed up into the wind and capsized.

But Sarby and de Jongh were ahead of me and the next time upwind I lost distance on them. I had gone downwind with only the small reefed mainsail and I lost so much when we went upwind that I realized that on the dead run I had to do something. I was losing but I kept my third place at the windward mark and then I hoisted the jib on the dead run and put out the whisker pole and found I was gaining because I kept the boat straight and I had the feeling I had a little better balance than the others.

I took the jib down again at the lee mark and then I saw that I was not losing upwind so it must have been blowing even harder on that round. I put the jib up again on the last two reaches and was gaining quite a lot and de Jongh was then leading. Then when Sarby started

"... de Jongh came past ..."

"... he luffed ... and capsized."

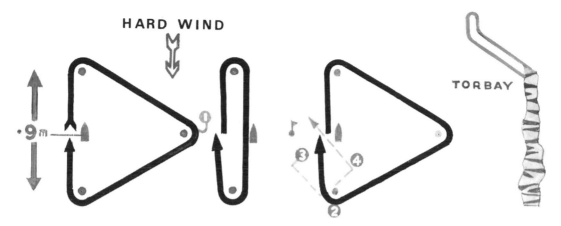

HARD WIND

TORBAY

·9m

The Olympic course for the last race at Torquay showing the three separate rounds. At 1 Herbulot capsized. At 2 Sarby capsized. At 3 de Jongh filled and was bailing. At 4 Paul tacked on a wind shift and crossed the line ahead.

The Gold Medal

the last short beat I couldn't see him anymore. Then I saw under my boom that he was capsized.

O.K., now I was second and de Jongh continued on the same tack but I tacked immediately to go into Torquay and get smooth water. On the way I saw that de Jongh was going very slowly and something must have happened. I could not see what was wrong but he was very, very slow and then I got a windshift. I tacked and now I was sure to be ahead of him, and then he stopped completely and was bailing.

Afterwards he told me when he tacked he had capsized and got the boat full of water. When I passed him I eased the mainsheet a little and then was *very* careful. I was not even hanging out completely because the toestraps could break and I was being so careful. I knew the Gold Medal was mine but de Jongh had to finish so that the American was lower than No. 3. He was bailing but when Morits Skaugen of Norway came closer to him he had finished bailing and he took the main and jib sheets in and passed the line. Skaugen was third, Castellanos from Uruguay was fourth and Evans of America was fifth. Sarby bailed out and finished 14th.

But thinking about preparing again—the evening before the last race I was concentrating on everything that might happen and that's really, I should say, a disadvantage. At that time, I wanted very much to win and I concentrated too hard by thinking out what could happen so that I should be prepared for everything. At that time in Torquay I

"... he stopped and was bailing."

1948 OLYMPIC GAMES—LONDON (Torbay)

6-metres

1. *United States, H. Whiton*   *4, 1, 1, 3, 8, 1, 2*   *5472.*
2. *Argentine, E. Sieburger*   *3, 3, 3, 2, 1, 4, 1*   *5120.*
3. *Sweden, T. Holm*   *5, 2, 2, 1, 3, D, 11*   *4033.*
4. *Norway, M. Konow*   *3217.*
5. *Great Britain, J. H. Hume*   *2879.*
6. *Belgium, L. Franck*   *2752.*
7. *Switzerland, H. Copponex*   *2594.*
8. *Italy, G. Reggio*   *2099.*
9. *Finland, E. Westerlund*   *1691.*
10. *Denmark, T. La Cour*   *1648.*
11. *France, A. Cadot*   *1280.*

Dragons

1. *Norway, T. Thorvaldsen*   *1, 2, 12, 1, D, 3, 3*   *4746.*
2. *Sweden, F. Bohlin*   *2, 3, 2, 2, D, 12, 1*   *4621.*
3. *Denmark, W. E. Berntsen*   *3, 4, 3, 5, 2, 5, 2*   *4223.*
4. *Great Britain, W. Strain*   *3943*
5. *Italy, G. Canessa*   *3366*
6. *Finland, R. Packhalen*   *3057*
7. *Argentine, R. Sieburger*   *2843.*
8. *Holland, C. Jonker*   *2508.*
9. *Portugal, J. F. de Silva Capucho*   *2123.*
10. *France, M. de Kerviler*   *1743.*
11. *Belgium, A. Huybrechts*   *1549.*

Stars

1. *United States, H. and P. Smart*   *4, 1, 2, 1, 3, R, 6*   *5828.*
2. *Cuba, Dr. C. and C. de Cardenas*   *7, D, 7, 2, 7, 1, 2*   *4949.*
3. *Holland, A. Maas and E. Stutterheim*   *3, 5, 5, 3, 4, 2, 7*   *4731.*
4. *Great Britain, D. Knowles and S. Farrington.*
5. *Italy, A. Straulino and N. Rode.*
6. *Portugal, J. Fiuza and J. Gourinho.*
7. *Australia, A. J. Sturrock and L. A. Fenton.*
8. *Canada, N. Gooderham and A. Fairhead.*
9. *Spain, J. A. Allende.*
10. *Greece, G. Calambokidis.*
11. *France, Y. Lorion.*
12. *Finland, R. Nyman.*
13. *Austria, G. Obermuller.*
14. *Brazil, J. Braconi.*
15. *Switzerland, H. Bryner.*
16. *Argentine, J. Piacentini.*
17. *Sweden, B. Melin.*

Swallows

1. *Great Britain, S. Morris and D. Bond*   *3, 1, 3, 1, 2, R, 4*   *5625.*
2. *Portugal, D. and F. Bello*   *1, 4, 4, 5, 1, 5, 1*   *5579.*
3. *United States, L. Pirie and O. Torry*   *5, 9, 5, 3, 11, 1, 2*   *4352.*
4. *Sweden, S. Hedburg and L. Matton.*
5. *Denmark, J. Rathje and N. Petersen.*
6. *Italy, D. Salata and N. Roncoroni.*
7. *Canada, J. Robertson and R. Townsend.*
8. *Norway, O. Christensen.*
9. *France, J. Lebrun.*
10. *Brazil, V. R. Ferraz.*
11. *Holland, W. de Vries Lentsch.*
12. *Uruguay, C. A. Saiz.*
13. *Eire, A. Delaney.*
14. *Argentine, J. Cibert.*

Firefly Dinghies

1. Denmark, Paul Elvström   R, 6, 3, 11, 5, 1, 1   5543
2. United States, R. Evans   2, 3, 13, 9, 1, 5, 5   5408
3. Holland, Koos de Jongh   6, 5, 17, 4, 3, 3, 2   5204.
4. Sweden, Rickard Sarby   8, 1, 7, 1, R, 11, 14   4603
5. Canada, Paul McLaughlin
6. Uruguay, F. S. Castellanos   14   Italy, L. Spanghero.
7. France, J. Herbulot   15.   Finland, E. Palmgreen.
8. Belgium, P. van der Haeghen   16.   Eire, A. Mooney.
9. Gt. Britain, A. McDonald   17.   Argentine, Y. Brauer.
10. Switzerland, A. Oswald   18.   Australia, R. French.
11. Brazil, W. Richter.   19.   Spain, J. A. Allende.
12. Norway, M. Skaugen.   20.   South Africa, H. McWilliams.
13. Portugal, J. M. Tito.   21.   Austria, H. Musil.

Gold Medal victory smile. Paul putting the Firefly *away after winning at Torquay in 1948.*

39

didn't have the trouble with the nerves that I got later, but preparing like this can make a man too nervous. But that time it was fun because nobody expected I should win and it was also fun because I tried some-thing I never tried before. So that time winning was really wonderful.

The trouble with me was that already I prepared for winning the next Gold Medal the day after I had won the first one. My feeling was that if I could have held the *Firefly* upright in Torquay I would nearly win every race, because the main problem for most people was that they were not clever enough to balance the *Firefly*. They were sitting up and half-hanging and you wouldn't see anyone with the hanging technique

The training bench with a weight to simulate mainsheet pull.

we are using today. So the same winter after the '48 Olympics, some few days after I came home I made a piece of a deck, what we now call the training bench that everybody now uses who is interested in getting fit. Then I used sandbags on my chest and practised hanging but I had my knee outside the gunwale. It was hard but it got the most weight out over the side. I worked at that until I got my Finn in '51.

The Scandinavian Union had selection trials and they were choosing another boat than the *Finn* but later they changed their minds and we had the *Finn* for the '52 Olympics at Helsinki. In spring 1951 I had my first *Finn* and we had the first Scandinavian championships in Stockholm where I had a traveller track only one foot long.

Nobody knew how to sail with an unstayed mast. I had no experience at all of this kind of rig, but the Swedes used it on their canoes. I came second in the first Scandinavian championships after Sarby. My mast was stiff because I had the feeling that you would only be able to point with a stiff mast and it's weight was 13 kilos (29 lbs) and the minimum was $10\frac{1}{2}$ kilos! At the same time as having a short traveller I was hanging with my knees outside the gunwale and I remember that in the Sound where we had six Danish boats and two Swedish I won everything and was so much faster than everybody else, so I thought I could easily win in Stockholm.

"... I was hanging with my knees outside ..."

We started on a reach and I was playing because I thought that when we came to start upwind I would easily leave them all. But I realized that I was 4th or 5th in speed and that gave me a shock. They were faster because of my stiff mast, and also because the others had a hook on each side of the cockpit and they could put the sheet round the hook on the lee side to take the boom more to lee. I said to Sarby, "Rickard, you have much more experience than I have in this kind of rig, could you tell me why you are sheeting it out to the side?" But whenever I asked him he just said "I think it is better to do it that way".

No other explanation.

After the Scandinavian championships where I finished second I went back and lengthened the traveller and planed down the mast. These masts were really *very* stiff. Also I asked the local sailmaker to make a fuller sail which was absolutely maximum size. At this time the sailmakers were not very precise and they normally made a flat sail which was under the maximum dimension so that it would never be too big. With these changes I felt the boat was going better and the next year we had the Scandinavian championships in Denmark. That was the Olympic year and we found that we were now so much faster than the Swedes.

Now that we had the *Finn* I was sailing all the winter. In the autumn of '51 I was sailing every day with Helmar Petersen. He now lives in New Zealand and won the Gold Medal in *Flying Dutchman* in Tokyo. We were sailing for one month every day for 5 to 8 hours and

"... round a hook on the lee side ..."

we became so equal that if he started first he won, if I started first I won. And so the next Scandinavian championships in '52 before the Games I won with five firsts and one second and he was second with five seconds and one first. But there was no competition. There were no Norwegians. There were the Swedes and the Finns but Sarby wasn't there.

In winter time I was sailing on Saturday and Sundays and in summer time I was sailing every single day. I could *play* with that *Finn* under all conditions. On the radio before the Games in Helsinki and after winning the Scandinavian championships we spoke about the classes that were in the Olympics and I was telling them that we didn't know anything about the *5·5-metre* because we had not been sailing in international competition. In the *Dragon* class, I thought we had a very good chance of a medal and in the *Finn* I could not see how we could lose. They must have thought I was very big-headed, but I was not really. I was so well prepared that I felt there wasn't anyone who could beat me. And I think that when you have no inferiority complex it helps you along.

Of course, at that time I was not clever enough to know how important it is for the mast and the sail to work together. I could have drawn a bad combination but I thought that I, myself, was so clever that whatever I got I could win. And in tactics also I felt I was the best. I was always thinking of racing so I was always thinking about what could happen in a race and when you are racing every day in summer time you get a lot of experience. I was the fastest but when we were training I was always starting last and sometimes I didn't win.

In Helsinki I had a faster speed than anyone else because I had the feel of the *Finn*. I also had an extra long traveller but we didn't have wind enough to use it but I got permission to put it in and it would have been a fantastic advantage if the wind came. The boats had a $1\frac{1}{2}$-foot track on top of the thwart and I had a longer one like today behind the thwart. But even at Helsinki I realized that I ought to make it longer for the time when the wind would have been stronger.

Peter Juul

Paul talking to Koos de Jongh, Bronze Medallist at the 1948 Olympic Games.

44

Paul trying out the Finn *which he drew in the 1952 Olympics at Helsinki. Note how very flat the sail is by modern standards.*

45

Jaques Lebrun of France saw that I had a wider traveller and he said to me, "You are a very good helmsman but it is not fair that you are sailing with a wider traveller". Of course he was right and he asked the Committee to disallow it so I changed it for the last two races. I can tell today that I had no advantage from it at all because I never used it so wide since the sail was so flat. Remember that the more baggy a sail is the more you have to sheet it outboard.

French Olympic sailor, Jacques Lebrun won the Gold Medal in the single-handed class in 1932 at Los Angeles, and has sailed in almost every Olympic Games since, and still sails actively in the 5-0-5 Class.

A. Traverso

An amusing thing happened in one race when I tacked and, by accident, I missed the toe-straps and so I dropped into the water. At that time I was lying third but, as I fell into the water, I still had the main sheet in my hand, so I came very fast up again and continued. I was wearing a lot of sweaters so I found I was very heavy, but I was gaining in speed and it didn't take a long time before I was first. It was the extra weight of water which helped me, so by accident I became faster in that race. Now, of course, everybody knows that, but at that time they didn't realize it.

In another race I started too early, and I couldn't get back because I had boats on each side. So I eventually started far behind the others and, at the first mark, I was the boat before the last. On the two reaching legs, I gained at least twelve boats, because they all went in a circle instead of straight to the mark.

I am sure the reason why many skippers go too far up to windward on the reaching leg is because they don't realize that to look straight ahead of a boat you have to look a long way to the windward of where you think you are.

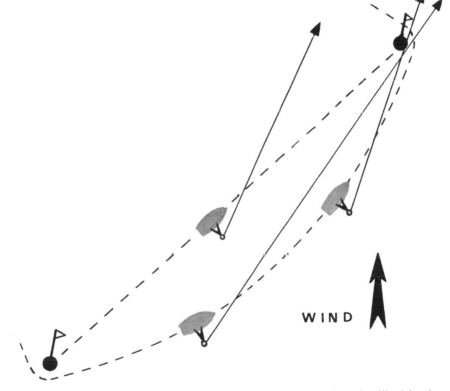

WIND

You can draw it with a pencil and you can see how it will mislead you if you don't have any guide line. The same sort of thing happens on the starting line, when you are starting in the middle of the line and you've got no transits. Always start a little bit farther to windward than you think. You feel you are on the line when you really haven't quite got there.

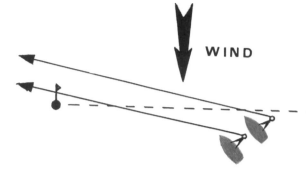

W I N D

The main tactic is when you are reaching that if you want to go straight you should have the feeling that you are going to the lee side of the mark, and then you are steering exactly on the mark, and it is very important, especially when planing. Most planing boats, when they come to the mark, are nearly on a dead run for the last hundred yards.

And then, when we started beating, again in this race the leaders all went toward the shore and when I came round the mark, far behind, the leading twenty boats had sailed into no wind and so, of course, I tacked immediately and was lucky to get clear of that hole. When I was sure I could pass the group, I tacked again to starboard and passed them all except Willie Pieper from Switzerland but my speed was so much better than his that I took only four more tacks to get ahead of him. At that time I was gaining at least one boat's length on him every time we tacked.

That shows the value of training, of course, and the earlier bit of luck shows the value of keeping your eyes open.

It's a fundamental rule that before I went to any championship, I was sailing 8 hours a day. I was always blaming the keelboat sailors that they shipped their boats early and were not sailing immediately before they came to the Games. I also had nearly two seasons and one winter of training in my own *Finn* before I went to the Olympics at Helsinki. I had been training all winter, hanging out on the training bench with sandbags on my chest, and I found that I could wear sweaters and put them in water before the start if the wind was strong enough, so that I could be heavier. All this I did because of the experience I had in Torquay in '48, where I found myself like a mosquito, not being able to keep the boat upright. But if I could do so well without any training and with such a light weight in Torquay, then I was nearly sure that, after four years' training and four years of thought on how to sail a single-hander, that I would win again, and I was right. I had almost three thousand more points than the No. 2 in that Olympics and in the race that I started too early I was far behind but the next time I came to the windward mark I was first. I had the feeling that I would have to be very stupid to lose.

"... I missed the toe straps. ..."

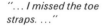

1952 OLYMPIC GAMES—HELSINKI

6-metres
1. *United States, H. Whiton*   *4, 9, 1, 1, 8, 3, 1   4870*
2. *Norway, F. Ferner*   *1, 4, 2, 4, 10, 1, 5   4648.*
3. *Finland, E. Westerlund*   *3, 6, 3, 5, 1, R, 3   3944.*
4. *Sweden, S. Salen.*
5. *Argentine, E. Sieburger.*
6. *Switzerland, L. Noverraz.*
7. *Canada, W. Gooderham.*
8. *Italy, E. Poggi.*
9. *Great Britain, K. Preston.*
10. *Germany, W. Elsner.*
11. *U.S.S.R., N. Ermakov.*

5·5-metres
1. *United States, Dr. B. Chance*   *4, 1, 10, 11, 3, 1, 1   5751.*
2. *Norway, P. Lunde*   *2, 5, 2, 2, 10, 2, 4   5325.*
3. *Sweden, F. Wassen*   *1, 10, 1, 3, 7, 9, 13   4554.*
4. *Portugal, D. Bello.*
5. *Argentine, R. Vollenweider.*
6. *Great Britain, S. Perry.*
7. *South Africa, S. Horsfield.*
8. *Finland, H. Dittmar.*
9. *Germany, H. Lubinus.*
10. *Italy, D. Salata.*
11. *Denmark, P. Ohff.*
12. *Switzerland, H. Copponex.*
13. *Holland, W. de Vries Lentsch.*
14. *France, J. Roux-Delimal.*
15. *Bahamas, D. Pritchard.*
16. *U.S.S.R., K. Alexandrov.*

49

Dragons		
1. Norway, T. Thorvaldsen	2, 1, 9, 1, 6, 6, 1	6130
2. Sweden, P. Gedda	5, 3, 3, 2, 5, 1, 3	5556.
3. Germany, T. Thomsen	4, 8, 6, 3, 1, 3, 2	5352.
4. Argentine, R. Sieburger.	11. United States, W. Horton.	
5. Denmark, O. Berntsen.	12. Australia, A. Sturrock.	
6. Holland, W. van Duyl.	13. Great Britain, T. Somers.	
7. Brazil, W. Richter.	14. Finland, E. Fabricius.	
8. Portugal, J. Tito.	15. U.S.S.R., I. Matvejev.	
9. Italy, G. Carattino.	16. France, M. de Kerviler.	
10. Canada, J. Robertson.	17. Belgium, J. de Meulemeister.	

Stars		
1. Italy, Staulino and Rode	2, 1, 2, 2, 1, 2, 1	7635.
2. United States, Price and Reid	1, 7, 1, 1, 3, 1, 8	7216.
3. Portugal, Fiuza and Andrade	4, 8, 3, 3, 5, R, 3	4903.
4. Cuba, C. de Cardenas.	13. Great Britain, B. Banks.	
5. Bahamas, D. Knowles.	14. Austria, H. V. Musil.	
6. France, E. Chabert.	15. Greece, T. Razelos.	
7. Sweden, B. Melin.	16. Argentine, J. Brauer.	
8. Holland, A. Maas.	17 U.S.S.R., A. Tshumakov.	
9. Switzerland, H. Bryner.	18. Australia, B. Harvey.	
10. Canada, J. Woodward.	19. Finland, R. Nyman.	
11. Germany, P. Fischer.	20. Jugoslavia, M. Fafangeli.	
12. Brazil, T. de Paula.	21. Monaco, V. de Sigaldi.	

Finn Monotypes		
1. Denmark, Paul Elvström	1, 5, 1, 1, 3, 4, 1	8209.
2. Great Britain, C. Currey	9, 10, 8, 8, 1, 2, 6	5449.
3. Sweden, Rickard Sarby	6, 1, 4, 6, 10, 12, 14	5051.
4. Holland, Koos de Jongh	4, 2, 5, 11, 5, 10, 9	5033.
5. Austria, Wolf Erndl	17. Portugal, M. Quina.	
6. Norway, M. Skaugen	18. Belgium, C. Nielsen.	
7. Italy, Adelchi Pelaschiar	19. Finland, K. Kallstrom.	
8. Canada, Paul McLaughlin	20. Uruguay, E. Lanz.	
9. Brazil, A. E. Bercht	21. Eire, Alf Delaney.	
10. Spain, R. Balcells	22. Australia, P. Attrill.	
11. France, Jaques Lebrun.	23. Jugoslavia, K. Baumann.	
12. U.S.S.R., P. Gorelikov.	24. Cuba, J. de Cardenas.	
13. Switzerland, Willy Pieper.	25. Argentine, C. Benn Pott.	
14. Bahamas, Kenneth Albury,	26. Greece, A. Modinos.	
15. Germany, W. Krogmann.	27. Japan, K. Kaitoku.	
16. South Africa, Helmut Stauch.	28. United States, E. Melaika.	

50

At the Scandinavian Championships at Karlstad in 1952.

Three

Family and business

The first *Finn*

Paul. I first got a *Finn* in 1951 and that year I went to Kiel to race in the *Finn* class. That was quite interesting because we were only about ten *Finns* and the old 1936 *Olympic Monotype*, the *O-jolle*, which was a bigger boat, started ten minutes ahead of us. I had no competition in the *Finn* class so I worked for beating the first *O-jolle* each day. And sometimes I beat him by two minutes plus the ten that I had given him at the start.

And it was at this time too that I married my wife Anne. One day soon after we were married I remember that she was holding the bow of the *Finn* and fell though the pier and grazed her legs. We were carrying the boat and so I said "Is the boat all right?" and she became so angry because her leg was badly scratched.

How many times have we heard similar stories? We are all the same with our boats. Anne Elvström knew from the start that she had got competition!

At this time Paul was in business as a house-builder. He had a couple of foremen and employed casually whatever men he needed. He built up the business successfully but it was never more than a casual temporary affair and, as Paul said later, had no cash value. In fact, after the Helsinki Olympic Games in 1952 he had to do National Service in the Army for eighteen months and during this time he completely stopped his business.

On his return in 1953, Paul re-started the building business and it provided a reasonable living for Anne and himself. But he was taking every opportunity to race dinghies and it was around this time that he began to wonder if a secret wish of his could at last be realized.

Paul had always wanted to make his own sails. Even from his earliest days in the Oslo-dinghy he knew the vital importance of sail shape and later, in the Dragon, he had reason to be acutely conscious that his sails were poor but too rotten to be capable of alteration. A new Ratsey genoa had showed dramatically the value of a good sail.

Now that Paul had got his building firm on to a sound basis and some money was coming in, all his thoughts and energy turned to the problem of making sails. It seemed to him that here was a facet of yacht racing which was capable of vast improvement. He had many times tried to get other sailmakers to execute his ideas with results ranging from inability to translate his ideas into practice to point blank refusal to make such radical changes in an age-old art.

Paul felt that it was not possible for a beginner in sail-making at that time to make a living and he had his wife to support and soon the first of his four children was to arrive. Nevertheless, he could not restrain the urge to make faster boats and to make existing boats go faster, and the sail was vital since it provided the motive power. He went to a famous Danish sail loft and he asked if they would let him make a sail on their floor and they agreed. So Paul made his first Finn sail and it proved to be quite fast—certainly faster than others at that time because at the Scandinavian Finn Championship in Norway his worst result was a first place win by a margin of only two minutes! His best win was by fifteen minutes and so there was no need for tactics or anything—he just had to sail round the course. This was in 1953 and in the next year he took the fateful decision to start up sailmaking on his own.

Paul went to his old school friend, Erik Johansen, universally known as "Strit", who was at that time sewing up trousers in a factory. "I told him that we should make sails because we feel we know what shape a sail has to be. So let us start because I have money from my company. So we started with this money and then really we were lucky because we were not knowing anything about cloth. We only knew how the sail should be when it was ready and we were lucky to find a good cloth and so the sails became much faster than we expected."

The first problem was that Strit Johansen had to eat and so Paul had to guarantee his wages from the proceeds of the building firm until some profits were made. Secondly Paul realized that there was too much hand-work in the traditional method of sailmaking—it had to be mechanized as far as possible.

Immediately he made two main advances in technique. He found an old sewing machine designed for putting soles on to boots and shoes and adapted it to sew the bolt ropes directly onto the sail. Tradition said that the roping tension was vital to performance but Paul did not believe it. He wanted to design his sails in another way and only use the rope to hold the sail on to the mast via the luff groove. The rope was only for this purpose.

The other advance was a small machine for tracing parallel lines on the bolt of cloth with from six to eight pencils and coupled with this was a folding attachment. The sewer only had to follow the line and a perfect seam resulted.

Paul always has said that to win races you have to have luck and this was certainly true of his beginnings in sailmaking. There were three main things which, when added to his single-minded determination and his inventiveness, got his new business off the ground. These were firstly the accidental effects of his decision to sew his cotton sails with narrow cloths and secondly the type of cloth which he used, and thirdly the initial success of his first batch of *Pirat* sails.

Paul. There was nothing very special about my first sail in 1953. It was like we have today—rather full. All the other sails at that time were very flat. They were made with very wide panels and the cloth was not of the best type and so the diagonal elasticity was big and in strong winds they became too baggy. I had four-inch panels in my sail but it was

This cotton Elvström Finn *sail shows the narrow 4-inch panels and the considerable tapering near the tack.*

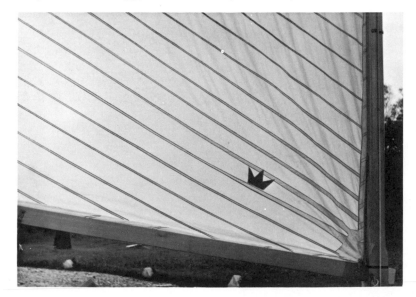

The first *Finn* sail

only later that I found that it helped reduce the diagonal elasticity. I made it in the first place because it looked nice. It was an accident that they were so fast. Because of this control it was able to keep the flow near the mast. The cloth also was good and this too was an accident. It was Italian woven cloth but not meant for sails. I don't know what it was for, but it was good and it was not only in the *Finn* class. We got the whole of the *Pirat* and *Snipe* classes because these sails were so much faster, especially in strong winds because of the cloth and the narrow panels.

Hans Fogh, the flower grower, whose early success in the Pirat *class gave Paul's sail loft a boost.*

A. Traverso

Strit Johansen was a *Snipe* sailor and so the very first Elvström sail was for his *Snipe*. But it was the *Pirat* sails which really set the Elvström sail loft on the road to success. The second sail went to a young Dane who was then quite unknown in the immensely popular *Pirat* class and in his first big regatta he scored runaway wins in all the races. The *Pirat* sailors immediately assumed that the unusual sail was responsible for the boat's remarkable speed since they could not believe that a beginner could be so good. They all came to Paul's door demanding sails like it and Paul captured a huge market. The sailor who acted as catalyst was Hans Fogh, later to become Paul's production manager and now with his own loft in Toronto, Canada. Hans later won a Silver Olympic Medal and a World Championship as well as having several near misses. So maybe it was the *Pirat* sailors who misled themselves in those early days!

Ragnvalds Foto

The Pirat *dinghy was very popular in northern and eastern Europe, and lent its mainsail to the O.K.* dinghy.

Paul. So, in 1954 I started making some alterations to the ground floor of my house so that we could make sails. We started by taking the whole cellar and then we took the first floor in the house. We first found that all the hand work was too slow and expensive. We had to organize it so that we had money enough to make a living for my best friend "Strit", and to finance the capital, so we must produce sails in a way so that we don't spend too much time and I think we were the first to sew on the bolt ropes with machines. And for seams, because we had a panel every four inches, we designed a folder for the machine so that the girl only had to follow the line. And to put the guide lines on the cotton cloth we made a rolling machine with six to eight pencils and then we wound the cloth up and it makes the lines very exactly.

We had no tradition to follow. We used our own brains and of course the old sailmakers criticized us but after a couple of years they had to copy us. Today we are used to seeing people who are good in sailing becoming sailmakers *because* they are good at sailing and know how to look at a sail. But in those days it was the old type of tradition- alists who were sailmakers. I think I was one of the first to break that old law.

The first sail loft in the cellar of the house at Hellerup. When keel- boats' sails had to be made, they had to borrow the floor of the restaurant nearby.

I didn't make sails in order to become first in sailing. I was not thinking of that at all. If I had thought that then I would only make my own sails. No, we were proud to make better sails and I could never have a sail better than my competitors in the *Finn* class, for instance. If someone didn't like the sail, I took it and used it myself.

"... I once made a special sail ..."

I once made a special sail for the Finn Gold Cup at Copenhagen in 1959 and the idea was that I put the panels along the foot at right angles to the boom so that the bag from the boom shouldn't rise up. You know in a dacron sail it doesn't do that but in cotton sails it became absolutely flat on the boom and became baggy in the middle. That was the disadvantage with a cotton sail and so I put the panels at right angles to the boom at the lowest part and I was quite fast, but someone borrowed the sail after me and never went fast at all. So maybe it wasn't such a good idea. But I was always trying.

The first sail Strit made was a *Snipe* sail but we couldn't sew the
rope on and he did it by hand and when I saw that it took such a long
time I said we must find a machine which can go right through the
rope. There *must* be a machine which can do it. Then we found an old
machine from the shoe industry and if you saw that today you would
laugh. It makes such a strange noise—*tarra-tum, tarra-tum, tarra-tum.*
It worked—but, honestly, we were scared that one day the sail would
fly away from the rope, but we found later that it was very strong.

In those days there was a great mystery amongst sailmakers about
the way you sewed the bolt rope on. We said that the rope is only to
keep the sail into the groove and the shape must be made in the cloth.
And we were right. The other sailmakers hadn't really had the
experience in racing like we had. For instance you remember they asked
us to sail on a reach for three or four hours before sailing upwind with a
new sail. This was nonsense and we sailed on the wind immediately
to stretch the leach fast. And we were right again. We never spoilt any
sail in that way. But when we changed to terylene and dacron, then we
got the trouble, because that was something new and this time we
were *not* lucky. Everyone started at the beginning again and we were
not clever enough.

All this time there were about eight people working on the lower
two floors of the house but the rooms were too small. A *Dragon* mainsail could only be fitted in by going out through the door, whilst a
5·5-metre mainsail had to go one metre up the wall!

But the new loft had only been running for two years when Paul
made his first overseas expansion and it happened like this.

One of Paul's earliest sailing friends was the Frenchman, Pierre
Poullain. They had met at various early *Finn* meetings including that
fantastic annual event at Zeebrugge where the whole international *Finn*
circus met for four days of rough and tumble round the mud banks and
the tide rips of that bleak North Sea harbour each May.

In 1953 Paul was, as a result, invited to Pierre's club, the *Circle de
la Voile de Paris* at Meulan on the Seine, to take part in one of those
masochistic French exercises, a twenty-four hours' race in *Sharpies*.
Here he met Albert Desbarges, a *Star-boat* sailor who had a small sail
loft in Cannes in the South of France.

Desbarges was an idealist who wanted a really good loft and, to
cut a long story short, in 1956 "Strit" said goodbye to Denmark and
went with his family to run the loft in Cannes. Strit, Desbarges and

Poullain and Desbarges

Pierre Poullain became partners in Elvström Sails, Cannes, though some time later Desbarges sold his share to the other two.

At that time also Paul gave up running his building firm and went to work full time at the sail loft.

Anne had tried hard to persuade Paul to concentrate on the building business as his mainstay. Her argument was that Paul already had a nice little business and so why throw it all away and start something quite new which could easily fail.

But Paul now hated his way of life and not only did he have his mind set on making sails for a living but he also liked the idea of working at his home. At all events there was no diverting him from his course once set—a rule as true in business as it was on the water. Complications such as the arrival of his first daughter, Pia, in 1954, just before he started the loft made no difference—he had decided what he wanted to do and no one could influence him in any way.

Paul explains a point to his friend, Pierre Poullain, and others during the 1956 Finn Gold Cup at Burnham.

The family expands

Paul. In the beginning, Anne was very jealous of my *Finn* sailing, because it was really my whole life outside the family. I was nearly always away sailing and when my second child, Christine (Stine), was born before the last race in the *5-0-5* World Championship in La Baule, I remember I was lying in the bath and Pierre Poullain came in with a telegram which told me I had another daughter. Because my first child was a daughter I really, at that time, wanted to have a son and so I was crying a little and was a little sad but not for long, because I became quite happy after a few hours.

My next child was born the day before I went to the Ski-Yachting Regatta in Cannes. This was Gitte—another daughter. When Trina, my daughter number four, came I got a telephone call the day before the last race in the World Championship in *Flying Dutchman,* when I was in Florida. Honestly, I only had this last race in my mind. I was working out the tactics that we should do, so that when Anne 'phoned me I was not thinking of the baby. I did not ask how she looked or anything, and Anne said to me when I came home that she nearly smashed the telephone down and didn't want to talk to me any more because of the way I spoke that day. The reason was that I was concentrating so much and thinking of the last race and what we should do to keep our first place.

When I got one daughter after another I, of course, every time would have liked to have had a son but now, when I am more than forty, I do not think of it at all, and I don't miss having no boys. I always say that what I don't have I am sure to get later. When the daughters get married, then I will have four boys in my home and then come their children, so I think I will have boys enough!

But I often like to tell why I have only daughters—it's because I like to do something to make the dinghy sailors happy!

I think it is very true that if I had had a boy in the nervous days when I was so enthusiastic about winning races, I would have spoilt him and I would have forced him to sail more than he wanted. So in a way I think it is very good I didn't have a boy, but today I wouldn't mind, because I would never force him to do anything because that's the worst thing any parent can do. I have seen examples of very good yachtsmen whose parents had taken too close a part and too much interest in their son's results, and the parents have really spoilt the fun and good sportsmanship for that boy.

I think Anne is the best adviser for parents and on family relationships. She has been marvellous for me; she just looks happy, never mind where I finish. If I had been in a bad position, or if I had won, you couldn't really see any difference. If I won and I said, "Aren't you

61

Paul and his family happy?'', she would say, ''I am always happy when you are playing on the water'', and that's really the main purpose of this sport. We are playing on the water because we like it and we, who play on the water, should always be happy and our families should be happy just seeing us playing and having a nice time. Life is too short to be other than happy.

Anne Elvström congratulates Paul at Naples in 1960.

Nordisk Pressefoto

In 1960 an awful accident happened for Anne and me. We were on the way to Zeebrugge, in Belgium, to compete in the *Finn* racing on the 1st May. We went there every year and I remember we should call in at a boatyard to see some *Finn* masts in Jutland and they were, of course, not ready—boat builders are always too late—so we had to wait five hours before we could leave, and therefore we had to drive all night. In the early morning Anne was driving and fell asleep. I was lying in the back of the car and it crossed the middle of the autobahn and started swaying from one side to the other, and Anne couldn't stop it. I woke up, but couldn't do anything, and the car rolled over and then came up on its four wheels again, but Anne had gone. I went out on the right side, but I couldn't see her. I looked under the car, but I couldn't see her. I went over to the other side of the car, and found her four or five metres from the car, and this was, as everyone can understand, awful because the first thing I thought was that she was dead, but I found that she wasn't; but it was really awful because she was badly hurt.

On the way to the hospital, I was with her and I remember waiting outside the hospital later. I bought another car because mine was completely wrecked, and also my old wooden boat, *Bes,* and so I slept in the new car outside the hospital, waiting for information of what would happen to Anne. It was so awful that I remember that I promised myself never to race any more, and I was so shocked that I said I would never travel with a dinghy any more and I hated everything to do with sailing, because of this accident.

But after a week I became normal again, and found that all that I had said was only because of the shock of the accident to Anne. Nothing happened to me and if Anne had been unhurt too, I would only have said, "We have never tried this before".

When the yachtsmen in Zeebrugge got to know what happened, they sent flowers and good wishes to Anne, and those who passed Hanover on the way back to Denmark from Zeebrugge visited her and it was really nice to feel that you have friends. Here I must say, that nothing is so nice in the world as to have good friends and, when people ask me if I could choose where I would like to live, and I have been all over the world, I must say that I want to stay where my friends are, and it's the same for everyone in the world. Anne slowly became better and today she is all right except that she cannot taste or smell anything properly.

After this accident, my old *Bes* was completely smashed and so I took the wreck back on the trailer and burned it, because it was good

63

for nothing. With this accident finished a small adventure, because I got this boat in 1951 and I won a lot of Scandinavian championships in it and two Gold Cups. I was hard with her. Once, for instance, when I had a tank in the stern and I wanted to fix the rudder fittings, I smashed the whole tank with my feet and fixed it so that I could sail again immediately and in that way I was very hard. But when we were sailing, I talked to her as if she was living. When I became nervous I talked to her, saying, "We have managed to do that before, so let's go and do it again". I don't know, but I think that every singlehanded sailor talks to his boat, so as to feel that he is not alone.

I never made this boat smart. What was important was to make the toe straps perfect, and the rudder very stiff and not elastic at all, because that would spoil planing. When the rudder is strong and stiff you can play with the boat on planing better than with a soft rudder. The hull was not very shiny, the centre-board was of iron and it was rusty. I remember before the Gold Cup in Zeebrugge that I knocked the rust away with a hammer because using sandpaper was good for nothing — the rust was so bad. I felt that I wouldn't like to have a perfect boat myself because, in the Olympics, we would sail another boat and if I sailed a boat which was not absolutely perfect and the fastest boat, I wouldn't get the practice in being able to make a slow boat faster. Nowadays I do all I can to make my *Finn* fast, and I am kinder to my boats. I like to see a nice boat and so I have completely changed in that way.

As we all know, Paul's sailmaking business was a success and expansion inevitably followed. The first move was to a large house on the coast road running north. The small town of Rungsted was anxious to develop its tiny yacht harbour by infilling and excavating a shallow bank extending from the shore. They offered Paul the house overlooking this area on favourable terms hoping that the presence of his firm would attract sailing people and other interests.

The house was extensively altered to accommodate a much larger cutting area as well as workshops, stores and offices. There was also a big garden where boats from the Elvström boat factory further up the coast, were stockpiled. Many sailors visited Elvström Sails which was fitted up in the charming and attractive Scandinavian way with teak furniture and panelling, up-to-date equipment, and neatly laid out gardens and lawns.

The house on the coast at Rungsted, which became the second Elvström sail loft.

The sewing room at the Rungsted loft.

Finally, even the Rungsted loft became too small and Paul then built a completely new and ultra-modern sail loft at Kokkedal just 3 miles inland from Rungsted. This loft was opened in 1968 and is really the last word in efficiency coupled with working conditions resembling more a de-luxe hotel than the normal idea of how offices should be.

There are pale green fitted carpets everywhere, textured fabrics and matting wall coverings, pine panelled ceilings, pot plants and trailing vines and a superb canteen furnished and decorated in the simple and tasteful Danish manner.

The office equipment is the latest and best available including a

Part of the huge cutting and sewing floor at the new Kokkedal loft. The cutting tables on castors can be seen on the left and at the back.

highly sophisticated inter-com unit as well as telephone answering and recording equipment for a full 24 hours coverage.

The plan of the building is square and is arranged on two floors. At ground level the offices, canteen and packing rooms take up about one third of the area while the rest is an enormous workshop and store into which the trucks and vans can drive to load and unload in centrally-heated comfort, away from the bitter northern winter.

Up a central, open-framed staircase is the sail floor and the glassed-in production office. There are no windows, but natural light enters via translucent panels covering all four walls, and heating, as on the ground floor, is by means of overhead pipes and reflectors.

There is a row of sewing machines down one wall with specially designed chutes to take away the finished work by gravity. There is a hand-finishing area in one corner but the whole of the rest is open. Paul designed and built special cutting tables on wheels and each takes one sail or a group of identical sails one on top of the other and they are supplied in various sizes to deal economically with all the possible variations in size and shape. When not in use any spare tables can be pushed out of the way along a wall. The cutters work standing up, which is much easier than crawling about on the floor.

Finally, on the enormous flat roof is a crane which can lift boats up to *Soling* size and park them in rows. There is a boat from all the popular types up there so that sails can be tested initially on the actual boat and spars that they were designed for.

Paul has laid out flower beds and terraces around the building and you approach the front door over a bridge spanning a shallow pool. He owns a similar area of land alongside and there he plans to build a highly developed boat factory to replace the old wooden building at Humlebaek, some miles away. His intention is to build top racing boats starting with the *Finn, Trapez* and *Soling,* the first two of which have been in his production line for some time. Also he wants to have a showroom and retail shop for his products so that people can come and talk to the experts and buy everything they need from one place.

All the other Elvström sail lofts in Sydney, Bermuda, Cape Town, Cannes and Toronto are independently owned but they have the advantage of working technically together. They contact each other by means of a monthly report so that each is up-to-date in the latest developments in most classes. If any loft does not specialize in any particular class it can get information from one of the other lofts.

Financially these lofts are entirely independent and they can do what they like. They are only connected by friendship and the name but they have all the advantages in working together.

But though the sail loft has been an undoubted success and the boat factory is now at last showing possibilities after years of problems and setbacks there have been many other ideas which have flowed from Paul's restless and fertile mind. One of these was the Elvström bailer which he put into production in 1961 and which I promoted in Britain with the co-operation of the famous catamaran pioneer, Ken Pearce. Later the bailer was developed further and has now become a very big business all over the world.

67

Paul now talks candidly about the beginnings of the bailer and of various other ideas of his which were not so successful.

Paul. In '56, I went to Burnham to take part in the Finn Gold Cup and in the first race we couldn't understand how some boats could continue planing, because we had so much water in our boats that we had to stop and bail it out. But after the race we saw that the leading boats had suction bailers—these were the old "tube" bailers—and, of course, immediately we bought some and put them into our boats. The disadvantage of these bailers was that, if we forgot to pull them up, they bent when we took the boats ashore, and then we couldn't get them up at all.

Therefore, I got the idea that if the bailer closed itself by pulling the boat up, there wouldn't be any damage to it. It was also a disadvantage of the tube bailers that when we tacked, or when we were waiting for the starting gun, the bailer didn't work and we got a lot of water back into the boat through the bailer. So I designed the new bailer based on the experience of Rickard Sarby of Sweden, who had a homemade bailer which was very effective. I took his principle and designed a bailer of a wedge shape with a non-return flap, which could be commercially sold, and that was the start of an enormous production. Ever since then I have continued making improvements in the design because I had to make bailers for all types of dinghies and now keelboats too and for various hull thickness and so on. We now have five models for different boats.

I will never forget that, at the time I was thinking of the bailer, Colin Ryrie from Sydney came to Denmark with an Australian bailer. It was just two pieces of wood with a metal plate on top, and he was saying all the time that a bailer need not be expensive. He said, "Look at this. It works perfectly and I made it in half an hour!" It was fixed entirely on the outside of the hull and there was just a hole in the boat plugged with a cork. You then pulled out the cork and the bailer started to work. It cost nothing.

He put that bailer on a *Finn* in 1959 in Copenhagen, and we all laughed at it and when he took the boat out the first time, something hit the bailer and knocked it off and that was the last we ever heard of it.

I have always had a lot of ideas as to how a boat should be made, and I have had many unconventional ideas that I would be scared to make because they were so far from normal that I would be afraid to

Bello of Portugal designed a stainless steel bailer for Stars. It was very wide and shallow and it had a non-return flap. Also it was retractable and locked when closed with a lever.

Thomas Walker of England designed a little round projection which had a slit in the bottom. It bailed very slowly but it had a clever sealing system with a neoprene flap which was closed by a piece of cork which lifted it upwards.

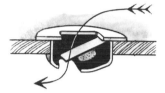

Jack Holt made a cheap and clever plastic flap bailer which got over the sealing problem when open by having the sides recessed into a wedge shaped slot. It bailed well but had no non-return flap.

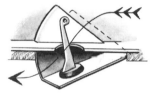

The first successful bailers in England were the tube type which were made by Lewmar, Gibb, Avon and others. They bailed rather slowly, had no non-return flap and were rather easily damaged.

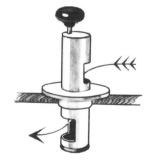

Sarby's bailer was rather like the Bello only much narrower and had a wide projecting flange.

My first bailer was half way between Sarby's and Bello's and was deep and fairly narrow with a non-return flap.

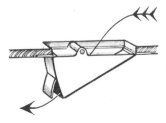

make something wrong. For instance, I think I was the first in the world to try to make a single-handed boat with a trapeze. I had certainly never seen it before, and people that I told my idea to thought I was completely crazy. So I made a very flat hull and just put a mast and sail on it, to see if it was possible for a man to steer and stay on the trapeze at the same time. The boat was so flat and low that when people saw it, they could only see the mast and sail and the man in the trapeze — quite funny!

*"... they could only see
the mast and sail and the
man in the trapeze ..."*

The idea worked, and I went to IYRU's trials for a new single-hander with a new boat which I had made in such a way that you could control it in all kinds of weather. But we had light and medium winds only and was not fast enough in my opinion. The boom was too low and I didn't like it myself and so I felt very stupid during those trials. I had the idea at the same time to make it into a two-man boat and it was so fantastically good that I forgot all about the single-hander and concentrated on making a very enjoyable two-man dinghy and I succeeded. This is the *Trapez* class.

70

The prototype Trapez *single-hander on the slip at Hellerup. Note the one-piece fibre-glass rudder and tiller and also the short, square dagger board, also in fibre-glass. The mast had to lean very far aft so that the helmsman was not pulled forward too much by the wire.*

I have sailed a lot of power boats. I had a little "stinkpot" to start with, and got a lot of experience. I changed it and rebuilt it several times, but I wanted then to make a self-righting boat and so I designed a power-catamaran, but this scared me in strong winds. It went very well, but I wanted to make it faster. I had a 110 h.p. "Z" drive motor in the middle, and then I put two motors, one in each hull, and it was very fast but, because the weight now came on each side, it was more dangerous on corners and I really got scared, so I gave it all up. This is really a typical example where I am gambling with ideas.

Many years ago, I think it was in '56, I had an idea of making a planing boat 19 feet long, 8 foot 6 inches wide, with a sliding seat of 15 feet and with 330 square feet of sail area. I worked at it for two and a half years and, when we came to trial sailing, I found it was so stupid that since we had a bonfire going in the garden, I put it on top. We also put a lot of old furniture and an old garden shed on top, and it made a very lovely fire. Then I did all I could to forget about that mistake, and I am only remembering it again now.

I also designed a sailing catamaran once, and I remember that it was so flat on the bottom that, when there was wind enough, it was planing. It was only a planing boat, tremendously fast in strong winds, but in light and medium winds, it was hopelessly slow. It also was always breaking its keels and so that was another mistake, but some time later I made a vee-bottom catamaran and in the north of Germany were built ten of them.

I was taking part in Kiel Week and Pierre Poullain from Paris was in Kiel too. On the day when we were not sailing, I suggested to Pierre that we go up and try the catamaran I had designed. I said to Pierre that he didn't need to take waterproof dress because it was absolutely dry on account of the vee-bottom. I was quite wrong, because we got water in the face all the time, and there was not one part of our whole body that was dry. Oh boy! I tried to forget that design, too!

All these boats I built for my own interest but this is the story of how I became a professional boat builder. There were some *Snipe* enthusiasts who had a boat yard near Copenhagen, and they had bought a lot of sails and owed me a lot of money. They could not pay me and the only way to get back any part of the money was to take some shares in their boat-building company. But the company went badly. It had started building *Finns* also and there was really no profit at all, and I had to take over the company and buy all the shares to

"...I worked at it for two and a half years ... and it made a very lovely fire ..."

continue and to be sure of being able to deliver the *Finns*. I felt very responsible for about forty *Finn* skippers who relied upon me and had paid fifty per cent of the buying price before they ever saw the boat. And so I became a boat builder and started "Elvström Boats".

I had a very big work to make the boat yard pay its way and we had a lot of troubles. But today it is going fine and I am building a modern new factory alongside the sail loft and we will build *Solings, Trapez* and *Finns*.

I must say that I criticize myself more than I do other people. When some other person has made a mistake in designing, I know how difficult it is to do the right thing, and so I don't criticize them too much. If I do something wrong I feel it very badly. I can nearly kill myself because people have bought something which I have made which is not perfect. I think it is a feeling in me that I have to do my best, and I must be the best. It is something I have had from childhood, so that, when I become involved in something, I want to succeed, otherwise I would prefer not to do anything or be involved in it at all.

Paul borrowed a One-Ton Cup boat and practised this way until it was ruled out of order.

74

Another time I thought I would like to see what ocean racing was like because it was something I had never done. I borrowed a boat and we tried it in local races and were going to sail it later in the One Ton Cup. We found it was too slow but the crew were so enthusiastic that we took it to Le Havre knowing we had no chance. There was another design which was so much faster.

Then a man who had a *"C" class* catamaran wanted to try to win the "Little America's Cup" and he asked me to sail the boat. We challenged the British but they did not accept us and the Australians sailed instead. After that I had no time nor any interest in competing again but the boat we had then was very fast.

This was a boat called *Opus* and we took it over to Sheppey to race against the British *"C" class* boats but they all disappeared and went to race somewhere else.

The only boat we could find was the Australian challenger and we did trials and found we were fast especially upwind. We saw in the reports later that it was the same with *Lady Helmsman* and I was satisfied enough to know that and so there was no reason then to try to challenge the year after.

The feel was something quite new to me and I had no practice so I felt that I could have been much faster. But I must say that racing between only two boats is not the sort of racing that I like.

My dream for the future is to go cruising with my family to all the nice places round our coasts. I am thinking a lot about trimarans, small ones and big ones, because I like the speed of these boats and I like the idea that you can go in very shallow water.

There are so many small places where you can't sail with a big keelboat. You can say that I could make a centreboard cruiser for sailing in shallow water but they are slow boats. I really only like fast boats but they must also give me pleasure to sail. The tiller must be lively and this is difficult with a multihull but I think a way will be found.

A semi-wing mast was tried on the Catamaran Opus. The minute jib was intended to help the boat when tacking, but it was not a success and a few minutes after the photograph was taken the mast broke. Later, a wide-wing mast was fitted and the boat proved extremely fast.

Four ————————————————————

Racing—1954 to 1956

Aage Birch

One of Paul's earliest sailing friends, and one who has, within his limited field, been an outstandingly successful helmsman, was the Danish *Dragon* sailor Aage Birch. Their friendship was a little unusual for Paul in that they were both very determined helmsmen and yet for several years they raced in Aage's *Dragon* with Aage steering and Paul crewing.

But Aage and Paul first became friends during the war when in 1943 and 1944 no sailing was permitted on the Sound between Denmark and Sweden. The *Juniorboats* had all been moved to a fresh-water lake called Furesøen some miles inland and it was on the shores of this lake that Aage Birch lived. Paul, during a talk with Aage, remembered some incidents whilst racing here during the war.

Paul. I will never forget, Aage, that we were sailing at the local club and in every race for one cup there were ten boats but it was only a fight between the two of us because you were nearly sure to win but what I remember was every time we started I went close to the starboard end mark and you went to the port end mark. You had worked out that when you came to the shore you could ask for room to tack, and every time I tacked and gave you water, and because of your better speed you just went past me and I never had any chance to catch you again.

You had two tall crews and you had more weight to windward than I had. Of course it made a difference but we cannot say if it made all the difference. One thing I remember was that every time you asked for water there was about four or five boat-lengths between us. So after these races I had the feeling that I should never have had to give

77

you water and then you would not have passed because when you tacked you would have had to bear away and go behind me.

I tell this only because during the race I was not sure if what you did was right or wrong. Now I know it and I will never forget that it was wrong of me to give you room. I should just have told you that you have to go behind me. You knew already at that time that when I gave you room it was good for you because you did not lose that boat-length.

Aage mentioned that he was born on this lake and he knew exactly where the wind shifts were in every wind condition. He knew he had unbeatable local knowledge on his home course.

Paul helped Aage Birch to build Aage's boatyard at the same time that he was at the architecture school. He made the drawings during the time that he had examinations so that any afternoon that he was unable to go out and build he was drawing for Aage. Then Paul and Aage built the boatyard together with their own hands. Aage closed the yard later and started making rubber boats but he has now finished with that business too.

Aage Birch had, up till the writing of this book, won the *Dragon* Gold Cup four times, in 1963 at Marstrand in Sweden, in 1964 at Travemunde in West Germany, 1966 at Copenhagen and in 1967 at Hanko in Norway. He had also won the Silver Medal in the 1968 Olympic Games at Acapulco and is therefore one of the greatest *Dragon* helmsmen of all time. In the 1966 Gold Cup there were over one hundred *Dragons* competing and it blew hard. Aage had always excelled in blowing weather and it will be seen shortly why this was so.

It was in 1954 that the Royal Danish Yacht Club asked Paul if he would sail for Denmark in the first of the postwar series of IYRU European Two-man boat championships. The racing was to be held at Rimini on the Adriatic coast of Italy and the hosts were to provide ten boats for the ten competing countries. The boats were to be changed after each of the ten races thus ensuring complete fairness.

The boats were to be those of the new *Flying Dutchman* class but they were very few outside Holland, Germany and Italy. There were none in Denmark and Paul had never seen one.

Paul. I thought I should have a crew who knew something about spinnakers and so I asked Aage Birch to come. He said, *"Flying Dutchman?* What is that? I have never seen one before"*, and I replied,

"No, but I think we go down one week before and then we can learn about it."

I remember that we took the train down and it was a long way without a sleeping compartment. In the train we were talking rather loudly and we spoke about a lady who was in the compartment and three hours later the lady asked us something in Danish so I realized that she understood everything that we said and I was really shocked. We didn't say another word to each other for an hour!

Aage. We arrived at last and saw all the nice new boats there and the next morning we went out very early.

Before we left the shore we asked what this belt thing in the boat was for. We didn't know before we left Denmark that we had to stay on a trapeze. I had never seen such an arrangement before. I remember it was only like a rope that I put around myself and it was not very comfortable.

We were two or three hundred metres out of the harbour when suddenly the water was closing over my head. The mast had broken and dropped me into the water and so we went back to the harbour again and the people there were very nice and said, "O.K. we have a spare mast. In fact we have five or six spare just in case of damage."

So we took a new one and put it in the boat and then in the afternoon we went out again and soon I found myself under the water again and you shouted to me, "Come up quickly. We have to have a new mast." So we went into the harbour but I don't think the smiles were exactly the same this time. When we got a new mast again we said we will go out again tomorrow.

The next day we said we would take a long trip down the coast to see what it was like to sail here. We went down with the spinnaker set and had a nice sail for about an hour down the coast, looking at the scenery and the water and everything and then we said, "Now we will start tacking and it will be good training for us."

After twenty seconds it was the same story and I found myself down under the boat again and you said this time, "Come up quickly. There is a shark after you!" and you were laughing when you pulled in the broken bits.

It was blowing quite hard and so we had no chance to paddle home. We took the *Flying Dutchman* to the shore and got one of the houses to telephone to the club and we said, "Here we are." They said, "Where?" and we said, "Oh! we do not know." So we ran out into the road and asked some people and looked at the shops so that at last we found out where it was. After half an hour or so they came with a car

79

and picked us up and took us back to the club and I was sure that they were thinking that if we went on like this they would not have any masts for the racing.

Paul. Then we tried to find out why it was that we were breaking the masts. We found that the spreader went right through the mast without any reinforcement or other fittings. When the mast bent the spreader twisted and opened the mast in the middle so that it broke.

So we went to a boat builder and told him how to make the fittings and after that the masts were O.K. I think that we saved the whole of the European championship for them. It would have been terrible if all the boats in the first race had broken their masts.

I remember Stewart Morris came from England and we were both very happy because we had heard a lot about him and we were really proud to race against him. There was also Roger Tiriau from France and Conrad Gulcher from Holland.

Aage. After this story we were very afraid for the masts and I was a little anxious when I stood out in the trapeze that I was going to swim again this day. But in the first race we were just rounding the tacking mark and I looked back and saw that the Dutch sailors were doing something. They were looking at the mast and then the crew was pushing it to the lee side with his leg because it was bending to windward.

The crew told me afterward that he had the thought that he was pointing better, but I thought that these people must be very clever because we would not dare to touch such a mast, even with one little finger! We were laughing when we saw it because we said that they did not know how delicate these masts were.

It was an odd starting line there. There was a little current and a little wind from the same direction every day. We found out that we could wait at the windward mark for a minute or more and so we went to the point where we wanted to start and sat there. We knew that whilst we were there nobody could take our place. The first day we went there one minute before, and the next day about one-and-a-half minutes before, and after that more, so that in the last race I think we were there about five minutes before the gun.

Paul. We made this tactic in the first eight races. After that I think we both became a little scared not to win the last two races but in the ninth race a boat started too early and got in our way and we did a bad start and in the last race it was blowing hard and we found we were not fast. We came third and fifth in these two races.

What was important I think for both of us was that we changed boats after every race. So we were really proud of what we were doing since it was not because of a well tuned boat. It was entirely the handling of the boat.

Aage. I still remember how we put up the spinnaker. We had never sailed with spinnakers in dinghies before so we did it in the same way as we did it in a *Dragon.* We put it in the bag and put it up on the deck and then hoisted the spinnaker out of the bag just as you do it in a *Dragon.* The Frenchmen did it better. They were watching us during the practice period and said to us that it was a funny way to put up the spinnaker. It was a slow way but it was the only way we knew.

Paul. Also we had no flag at the mast-head and we took the spinnaker down in one race when we were leading. We turned the mark and had to go on to a reach and I thought we should be quite close to the wind. But, at the same time as we turned the mark the wind changed and so we had the sail sheeted in much too hard for a reach and we did not know it. We didn't move at all and it took us twenty seconds to realize it and by then the others had nearly caught us.

That shows how a flag can help, especially for someone who is not familiar with the boat he is sailing. Remember that the *Flying Dutchman* was quite new for us. It was the first time we had sailed it and the *Flying Dutchman,* I must say, is a special boat.

Aage. I can still remember the nice feeling of being on a trapeze for the first time. It was fantastic to see from outside how this nice hull moved through the water. I think that everyone who is on a trapeze for the first time will never forget that.

Paul. After that we came back to Denmark and we sailed in Sound Week in your old *Dragon.* The Gold Cup was to follow but we only had spare time to sail in Sound Week and we won.

But the feeling we had when we came back to the *Dragon* was that something was wrong. It was so slow. I think that because of that we were working all the time so hard to get it going, and therefore we won. The old boat was very heavy and not very fast.

Sergio Sorrentino from Italy competed and I think there must have been thirty or forty *Dragons.* We won three races. It was just before the Gold Cup and you said you would not compete in the Gold Cup because the boat was not in your opinion up to standard. We laughed afterwards! Then we went to Fredericia for the first Danish championship. We were talking about whether it was allowed to put a trapeze on a *Dragon* or not. The sailors said that if anyone was so foolish as to trapeze on a *Dragon* then they ought to be allowed to do it. We tried it a little but we gave it up because we knew it was unfair and a big advantage. We only mentioned it there so that they had the opportunity of banning it which was done the following year.

We found out another thing there and that was how to put up a spinnaker on a reach. We were lying second and Henning Jensen was leading. It was blowing a good medium wind about 16 knots. Then we tried to pull our spinnaker pole just a bit clear of the forestay. I think about 4 inches clear and at once the boat started to go.

We had the genoa up too. I remember I was sitting on the deck and I said to Aage, "It is wrong that we are not using this big area where the genoa is. We must catch the leading boat so hoist the genoa—it must be right."

Then we were gaining and after the race everybody said that it was fantastic how we could gain with the genoa up. After that time they started to copy us and when we came out in international races the Danes sailed with the genoa set and then the other countries copied. It was a big success. It was mainly always the young people who came with the new ideas and we came with that idea.

At the time of the Helsinki games I had got a group of people together and I was training with them. In those days there was really nobody outside Scandinavia who was sailing *Finns* at all and so I knew exactly if I was the fastest. But afterwards I liked sailing the *Finn* so much that I continued and I was sailing every winter. I think because of this winter sailing that two of us, my neighbour Bjorg Schwarz and I, were sailing so much that we improved and improved the technique, the handling, the sheeting, the playing with the mast. Therefore, before the Games in Melbourne we were again sailing together all the time.

Bjorg Schwarz was a very good *Finn* sailor but he was always sailing with his nose on to the deck and he couldn't see anything. I must say that he was the worst tactician but he was fast. Normally I was leading and sometimes I had to go slower to be in contact with Bjorg so I used to whistle when he should tack. Once in Helsinki we came first and second in a Finn Scandinavian Championship and I told him where to go all the way around. But then Harald Eriksen of Norway learnt about the whistling and he played a trick on Bjorg by whistling at the wrong moment. Bjorg didn't know where he was going and Harald caught him up.

Harald was a very heavy man and he could sometimes sail upwind faster than me in very strong winds. We had very hard battles in *Finns*

82

Paul's neighbour at this time was Bjorg Schwarz who became his training partner.

Bjorg Schwarz

but always very friendly. In '56 he was at the Scandinavian Championship in *Finns* and Bjorg Schwarz was leading on points but they only had light and medium winds and then I came at the end to race in the last two races in strong winds. I went out and took two first places in the two last races and Harald got two second places and Schwarz two third places. They were using the old Olympic points systems and I took two first places which would have been Harald's if I had not competed in the last two races. Therefore, Harald would have been Scandinavian Champion if I had not come. He might have been very angry with me but he wasn't. I knew and he knew that I came only too late by accident and not to spoil his result.

I always had some friendly tricks with Harald. I used to say that he sailed like a steam-roller and I was trying to get him angry on the race course. Once in Marstrand before a race the wedge cracked my boom. I didn't say this to anyone but we started downwind and I was lying first and Harald second. Harald used to be so slow downwind but here he was lying very near my stern on my wave and I could not go fast because of the boom. He was so happy that he could stay there and I didn't say a word until we started going upwind again. Then I said, "Harald, thank you for staying there because my boom is broken and

83

that's the reason I'm so slow". He was so angry with himself that he did not go up and try to pass me because I could not have followed.

I think that a lot of the fun of racing is when you know your competitors so well that you can play tricks on each other but each of you knows that the other is going to try and play tricks and is just as clever about playing tricks back again. Of course, nowadays this business of playing tricks is treated really very seriously in the Olympics. Some crews take a lot of trouble to mislead their competitors for instance into thinking they are using some special sails or something and the others take a lot of trouble to go and get this special gear only to find afterwards when it is too late that it was a trick and the special gear is not being used by the champion and is no use anyway.

"... I was swimming with the boat about thirty metres to the mole ..."

In 1955 we had a tremendously hard-wind *Finn* regatta at Zeebrugge and in the last race it was blowing twenty metres per second (forty knots). Before the start I had to bear off for another boat, but he stopped his boat, and so I had to bear off more, until I was sailing by the lee. I capsized to windward and it was the old, wooden boat *Bes* No. D6, which had almost no buoyancy.

The boat sank, but I got it up and I went to the bow and was swimming with the boat about thirty metres to the mole. Then I was standing in the water all the time, so as not to be disqualified, and I lifted the bow to get most of the water out. Then I let the bow down again and was bailing with my hand until there was so little water that I could sail and let the bailers take out the rest. All the others had started and gone, but it was blowing so hard I felt I could finish the race and hoped I could get a position in the final order. Only eight boats finished and I was number eight.

In those days we had cotton sails and after that capsize my sail looked so awful because it had shrunk, and I had no speed. But all the other boats capsized, except the seven finishers and me, but if one boat more had finished I wouldn't have won the series. So I was lucky to be able to win, but it was so hard to get the boat in and to bail out that I could feel it at least a week afterwards. I was really tired, but it shows the energy I had in those days. I wanted always to win and I liked it afterwards because it is nice to do all that you can and then to succeed.

In every race, before and since, I have never given up except if I had no chance at all to finish. If there was the smallest chance, then I continued. In the European championship in Naples in the *Star* class, my runners broke the spreader in the first race. The runners got round a spreader and when I pulled the runners back it broke completely five centimetres from the mast. Normally you are finished after that but I managed to tack and I told my crew to go up with plastic tape and see if he could put the broken end on to the mast and fix it, so that it stayed there. He said, "I can't go up", and I said, "You shall! I will tip over the boat and then you can walk up the mast or the sail, and you have to do it." So he went up and I gave him the tape on the end of the whisker pole and he fixed it. Then we tacked but, because of the spreader being five centimetres shorter, the mast looked awful but I continued with the sheets eased and finished the race and got a position about number fifty.

After that race I had a nice feeling that I had worked hard. If I had retired because of the broken spreader, then the whole day would have

85

been spoilt; but it was fun to finish at all—never mind what place.

I had very bad luck later in that European Championship, but if I hadn't had that bad luck later, I would still have been in a nice place among the six first, even though all races have to count in the *Star* class.

".. and then you can walk up the mast and you have to fix it . . ."

**The first
Finn Gold Cup
1956**

In '56, before we went to Melbourne, we had the *Finn* Gold Cup in England. In the first race in a strong wind and very cold weather, we didn't understand how some boats went so fast and didn't stop for bailing or anything. Then we realized they had suction bailers in their boats, and immediately we bought some and spent all the evening drilling holes. At that time it was the tube bailers which we had, and after that we did better.

I remember I came to Burnham, as I thought well tuned and in a trial sail before the first race, I broke my mast. In those days we had no experience with making them and so we broke very many masts. I had to put in a stiff mast, and at that time we didn't know how to plane the mast or how to tune the mast to the sail. We just bought a mast, and that was that.

And we had no wedge for the boom either at Burnham, and so in the first race we learnt that we had to put bailers in, and in the next race we learnt we had to put a wedge in to keep the boom down. We had never thought that we could do that because we had the feeling we would break the boom immediately. We had very weak booms, and some people were even sailing with claw rings on their booms because there was a possibility of reefing. But it was fantastic that we had no idea how to plane the mast at that time.

The Belgian, Andre Nelis, Olympic Silver Medallist and Finn Gold Cup winner, who was such a close opponent of Elvström in the Finn class.

The Burnham regatta was very early and we had very cold rain and snow and André Nelis won and I came second and Brian Rowsell of England was third. I went home to get another mast and went to Zeebrugge for the races on 1st May. I only remember that I won easily in Zeebrugge and then, before we went to the Olympics, we went to La Baule in *5-0-5s*.

Pierre Poullain borrowed a boat and I sailed with him. We had marvellous racing, especially with Jacques Lebrun and Richard Creagh-Osborne with his long crew, Derek Pitt-Pitts, who were sailing their boat No. 4. I can't remember all the races, but I remember the last one, which was in a strong wind—a fantastic race between our three boats where we changed places all through the race. At the first mark, Jacques Lebrun was first, I was second and Richard was third.

87

We were the fastest on planing, but we capsized when Pierre fell off the trapeze, and so Jacques became the leader again. Then Jacques capsized, and so Richard was the leader. But Richard's boat was heavy and leaky, and so we both passed him, but then Jacques went to the wrong mark in a rain squall and we followed. Richard was the best navigator, and so we all arrived together at the last mark. Jacques rounded first, then Richard and then us. We tacked immediately, followed by Jacques and then Richard, but just then the wind freed and so we crossed the line in that order, with the others far behind.

But that was a very, very exciting race, where three crews played tactics together, and I shall never forget it, because it was the most funny and altogether the best race I have ever sailed.

I remember when Jacques capsized, he had the wind on the port side and we came on starboard and had to bear away for him, so there was a discussion afterwards, how the rules were in such a case. If Jacques was disqualified from that race, we would win the World Championship. There was no protest, but there was only a discussion, and I remember that inside I didn't like it but, because I would have liked to win, of course I was feeling it could be fun if he became disqualified because of that. But I must say that I was very happy nothing happened because it would have been a dirty way of winning. At that time the rules didn't say anything about capsized boats. That came later. I just mention this situation because it's something I remember. I think it was one of the most exciting races I have ever raced, because so many things happened, and right to the very end it was so close, and that's the way racing should be.

"... but we capsized when Pierre fell off the trapeze ..."

And then, because I was the best foreigner in the World Championship in the *5-0-5s*, I won a boat as a prize! I was so happy about that, and the boat came to Denmark when we were in Melbourne. Just before Christmas, after we came back from Melbourne, I went out sailing the boat, and my crew had never been standing in a trapeze before and so I said to him, "You take the helm, I'll take the trapeze". But the mainsheet was very stiff with ice, so he couldn't ease the mainsail. It was a strong wind and it was very cold weather, and we capsized, but I had remembered when at La Baule we had capsized and Pierre was flying out onto the mainsail. So, to avoid that, I unhooked the trapeze and let myself fall into the water, thinking that I could then catch the centreboard and raise the boat up. Stupid—but I had not had experience enough in trapezing a *5-0-5!* When I fell into the water, it was very, very cold and my muscles became frozen. I tried to get up on the centreboard and I don't know where the helmsman was, I couldn't see him.

The mast was lying horizontal on the water, and I couldn't get up on the centreboard—it was floating too high. Then I started to be scared and realized it was my last chance to come up, and I had no life-jacket and had a lot of wet clothes and sweaters on. I made a last great effort and got up on the centreboard and there I saw the helmsman in the water, and I told him:

"Now, when I get the boat up, you have to come in by yourself. I can't help you."

My muscles were dead from being so long in the cold water and when I righted the boat I was, I must say, floating into the boat on my stomach, and I had no strength at all. I had to lie down in the water in the boat but soon I became a little better so that I could help the helmsman in, and we sailed ashore with an absolutely slack mainsheet, because the sheet was stiff with ice. It was too dangerous to take the sheet in.

I was taken ashore, and I was very near to drowning. My shoulders were blue in a circle about three inches across. That's what happened and that shows how much strength I had used to get out of the water, with all those clothes on, and from that day I started working on the life-jacket. That's the reason we today have an Elvström life-jacket for racing.

At the Olympics of '56 in Melbourne, I was absolutely sure that it would be a fight between me and André Nelis of Belgium if we got wind. If we had no wind anything could happen. So I kept a good eye on André all the time.

Before the racing we had a lot of practice in quite strong winds, and I began to see that the American John Marvin was going to be good. He had only once been in a *Finn* before but he was really training hard at Melbourne. He had a good weight and he sailed so that he really meant to win.

One day I went out to show him that I was faster and to try to give him a little complex against me. We were planing and I took my centreboard right up and was really going fast on those waves. And I passed him easily.

Another day before the racing André Nelis came to me and said, "Paul, I think you will win a third Gold Medal." And then I knew that he had already given up, and this was a very big advantage for me, because I felt him as a very dangerous competitor especially if the wind should be light.

In one race André was lying first and I was second. He rounded the lee mark first and then I followed and normally I should tack and tack again and in that way clear my wind and try to be ahead, but I wanted to show him that I could outpoint and pass him without tacking — and I did it. I wanted to tell him that whatever he did I could still pass him. I think maybe it was for fun but after I had done that he would never cover me or do anything to try to stop me from passing. We were very close in speed in general but he seemed to be faster in light winds and was cleverer on windshifts at that time, but it was so seldom that we had light wind races.

In the first race at Melbourne it was blowing hard and I had to stop planing on a reach when I had just passed John Marvin of the U.S.A. I had a shock-cord pulling the aluminium centreboard down on planing, but the centreboard was pulled by the chock-cord off the pivot and so I couldn't get the centreboard up.

Downwind in Melbourne with the long waves it was dangerous if you couldn't raise the centreboard. I was so sure that I could go much faster that I just stopped and fixed it. I had the feeling that if the boat was O.K., then never mind if they passed me I could pass them again. That was the feeling.

After that I got two very bad races and I became very nervous after the third race and thought I had a run of bad luck. But what I felt was bad luck was not bad luck at all — I was stupid. But I became calm

90

when we got a good wind and, in the next four races, I won by about two minutes in every race easily, because my speed upwind was so much better. I was sailing steadily and a little faster than anyone else, and so tactically it was easy. And so that was my third Gold Medal.

1956 OLYMPIC GAMES—MELBOURNE

5.5-metres

1. Sweden, L. Thorn   5, 1, 1, 3, 2, 1, 2   5527.
2. Great Britain, S. Perry   3, 2, 7, 1, 4, 5, 3   4050.
3. Australia, A. S. Sturrock   4, 4, 2, 4, 1, 3, 4   4022.
4. United States, F. B. Schoettle.
5. Norway, P. Lunde.   8. U.S.S.R., K. Alexandrov.
6. France, A. Cadot.   9. South Africa, N. Horsfield.
7. Italy, M. Oberti.   10. Germany, H. Lubinus.

Dragons

1. Sweden, F. Bohlin   8, 2, 1, 8, 9, 1, 1   5723.
2. Denmark, O. Berntsen   1, 4, 4, 2, 2, 2, 6   5723.
3. Great Britain, G. Mann   4, 12, 8, 1, 6, 5, 2   4547.
4. Argentine, J. Chaves.
5. Australia, G. Drane.   11. U.S.S.R., I. Matvejev.
6. Italy, S. Sorrentino.   12. New Zealand, R. L. Stewart.
7. Norway, T. Thorvaldsen.   13. Portugal, Conde de Caria.
8. Canada, D. Howard.   14. Finland, J. Flinkenberg.
9. United States, E. H. Walet.   15. Bermuda, H. D. Eve.
10. Germany, T. Thomsen.   16. Singapore, E. G. Holiday.

Stars

1. United States, H. P. Williams   1, 5, 2, 1, 2, 2, 2   5876.
2. Italy, A. Straulino   3, R, 1, 3, 3, 1, 1   5649.
3. Bahamas, D. Knowles   2, 2, 5, 2, 1, 3, 3   5223.
4. Portugal, D. Bello.
5. France, P. Chancerel.   9. Australia, R. E. French.
6. Cuba, C. de Cardenas.   10. Canada, E. H. Pennell.
7. Great Britain, B. Banks.   11. Argentine, O. M. Lagos.
8. U.S.S.R., T. Pinegin.   12. Thailand, Prince Bira.

12 square metre Sharpies

1. New Zealand, P. G. Mander   2, 1, 5, 4, 1, 1, 2   6086.
2. Australia, Rolly Tasker   1, 2, 2, 1, 2, 2, D   6086.
3. Gt. Britain, Jasper Blackall   3, 7, 3, 2, 5, 3, 1   4859.
4. Italy, Mario Capio.   9. United States, Eric Olsen.
5. South Africa, J. A. Sully.   10. Brazil, A. J. E. Bercht.
6. Germany, Rolf Mulka.   11. Canada, A. F. Cameron.
7. U.S.S.R., B. Iliine.   12. Greece, S. Bonas.
8. France, Roger Tiriau.   13. Burma, Khi Pe Gyi.

Finn Monotypes

 1. Denmark, Paul Elvström   1, 8, 15, 1, 1, 1, 1   7509
 2. Belgium, Andre Nelis   6, 1, R, 2, 2, 3, 2   6254
 3. United States, John Marvin   2, 2, 8, 3, 3, 2, 4   5953
 4. Germany, Jurgen Vogler   R, 3, 2, 9, R, 4, 3   4199
 5. Sweden, Rickard Sarby   3, 5, 12, 7, 6, 6, 7   3990
 6. South Africa, Eric Bongers   12, 12, 1, 4, R, 5, 11   3912
 7. Italy, Adelchi Pelaschiar   7, 16, 3, 6, 10, 8, 10   3409.
 8. Canada, Bruce Kirby   5, 17, 6, 10, 8, 11, 6   3213.
 9. Bahamas, Kenneth Albury   15, 9, 16, 5, 4, 7, 9   3182.
10. Australia, Colin Ryrie   4, 13, 11, R, 7, 14, 5   2965.
11. Great Britain, Richard
         Creagh-Osborne   16. Eire, J. Somers Payne
12. U.S.S.R., Y. Chavrin   17. Brazil, Jo Roderbourg
13. France, Didier Poissant   18. Argentine, Estephan Berisso
14. Singapore, John Snowden   19. Burma, Maung Maung Lwin
15. Austria, **Wolf Erndl**   20. Fiji, John Gillmore

Commodore Mackenzie congratulates Paul on coming ashore after the last race of the 1956 Olympics.

Before the Melbourne and Naples Olympics I was really training a lot in *Finns*, and I had the feeling that the more I was sailing and the more I was training, in particular turning marks, tacking and beating, the better I became.

I think most of my competitors can remember if we were beating together that when we tacked I was gaining about half a boat's length to one boat's length each time, and that came entirely from training. During the years when I was not sailing *Finns* I could not do it. I was never gaining on tacking and was sometimes slower than the best ones when tacking. It was a very strange feeling, and it proves how important it is to train, but I never went out training just for the fun of sailing. I went out to try and see if I could do something better.

For instance, when it was blowing very hard, I went out and practised gybing, and when it was blowing so hard that I couldn't get forward to grab the main sheet or anything, I was training to gybe without touching the sheets, or by using only one part through the floor block. I was also practising how hard I could put in the wedge without capsizing and so on. If I tried to do the same today, I am sure to capsize—I don't have the balance.

Of course, there is also physical fitness and so we did training in the gymnasium, because if you become tired, your brain doesn't work any more. You are thinking too much of the fact that you are tired, and it takes your thoughts away from the racing. So the better your physical condition is, the more it will help you during racing. The physical condition is, of course, not so important as the brain, but it helps.

Improving in your handling of the boat, of course, can only be done by practice. You will also automatically get fit when you are handling the boat. We sailed at every possible opportunity when we came near to a big event or an Olympics. Even during the winter, we were sailing every Saturday and Sunday if there was no ice. The week before every important meeting—Gold Cup and the Olympic Games—I was on the water nearly eight hours every day, so that it was the boat and me working together as one smooth thing.

My advice is that you have got to spend all your time at it if you want to have a chance to win. But maybe a day will come when all the top competitors in all the countries concerned are doing that—we can see it in other sports.

Five

1957—Learning about *Stars*

1957 was really a fantastic year. After the Olympics in Melbourne I first went to South Africa, to Durban, to take part in the South African championship in *Finns*. They invited me and they sent an aeroplane ticket. When someone invites me and spends a lot of money on an aeroplane ticket and they show hospitality and so on, then I am always so scared not to be able to do what they expect and these kind of races make me awfully nervous. So I tried really hard to win and even though it was a hot climate and I sweated still I put on all the wet clothes to be sure to win. I won all the races I competed in, except one light wind race where I was second and another race where I broke my mast when I was leading. So I won the National Championship and I was happy, mainly because they got what they expected. I feel responsible to do my real best when people invite me.

Cuba in *Stars*   After Durban I was invited to Cuba to take part in the World Championships of the *Star* class crewing Albert Desbarges from Paris. Desbarges was a very wealthy man, so he paid for my trip and everything, but it was first time I had been sitting in a *Star* and we had no tuning race or anything. I worked as the tactician.

When I saw the *Star* I put in some toe straps, but the other *Star* sailors told me that it was not allowed to have them in the *Star* class, so I had to take them out again. So then I was hanging out and using the jib sheet and the runners. This was like we do today on a *Star,* but at that time it was very unusual. Normally they lay along the side deck on their stomachs.

I remember this series and in the first race we were about number ten—about, I say, because I can't remember exactly—but in the hotel next morning we were eating with some American *Star* boat sailors and we discussed who the winner would be. Most of them said, after

94

the first race, that it must be one of the first five persons in that race. The next race was on that day and we came first and were in a good place all the time.

In one start I told Albert Desbarges what to do and I said he was to go as close to the Committee boat as possible, because there was not much room. We were coming up to a perfect start and then suddenly he let the mainsheet go completely. I had the jib sheet, but I took the mainsheet home immediately because I had taken it home once and cleated it and told him to go close to the Committee boat, but he took it out of the cleat. At that time my temperament was very hard so, of course, I was shouting, "What are you doing?", and I took it home again and we came two metres later over the start and I said, "Why were you doing that?", and he said, "Gosh! I thought there was one minute more." Then we continued and we got the best start.

During the race it was interesting that he was lying on the deck, because he always did that, and then he was looking behind at something and every time he looked we lost some speed. So then I told him to feel the boat, because why did he think I was there? "You sail. I will tell you where to go." I said. After the race, which we won, he said, "I have never been so tired in a race and I have not seen *anything*." I must say he was steering the boat better than I could do it. He was very clever at it.

Teamwork in *Stars*
and *Dragons*

Now that race was a lesson which showed that the helmsman must have complete concentration on sailing the boat fast. In some boats if you are the skipper and you are steering, you cannot concentrate on sailing the boat and also see where everything is. It's too difficult to do both in a *Star-boat* and I think in a good *Star-boat* team there must be one man who is a clever helmsman, because in a *Star boat* you have to improvise and you must have a good helmsman, but to see where to go you must have a clever crew. This team work is important in all boats, but especially in a *Star*.

Let us say that the helmsman is so clever in that particular boat that he can feel the boat and it never stops for him; then he has time for tactics also. This helmsman will have to be clever enough to feel the boat, and his crew must understand how to adjust the jib and mainsail together, so that the helmsman doesn't have to think how much they shall be sheeted in or out. Then that helmsman has time for watching the wind and the sea conditions and so you can, in such a boat, have team-work split up to give each man what he is best at.

Take the *Dragon* in the last Olympic Games in Acapulco. I think that Buddy Freidrich's crew's team work was the main reason for winning the Gold Medal, because it was really a team.

Then in another race at Cuba I made a terrible tactical mistake, because I could not see the tide. We went out to sea and the tide was against us, and I realized it too late, so that we dropped to the middle of the fleet. But the funny thing was that all the leading boats did not know why they were leading. So on the next round they went out and I tacked immediately and continued and continued along the shore. And when all the others were out at sea ahead of us, I said to Albert, "Now we are third ... now we are second ... now we are first", and he said, "How can you know that?" "I know it because the others can't come in. The current is stronger in between, so they have to stay out there. They have no chance." And I was right. That was fun.

Lowell North of U.S.A. had the same points as us up to the last race, so that the winner of this race would win the World Championship. It couldn't have been more close and at the first mark he rounded half a boat's length ahead of us. But downwind he disappeared and to be sure to keep our overall second place we covered Duplin from Boston and he went the wrong way. We knew he had gone the wrong way, but we wanted to be sure of the second place and so we stayed with him. We should never have done that because North went the right way and didn't cover us because he knew we had gone the wrong way. Then the shackle holding the mainsheet block on to the boom broke and, if we had only followed him, we would have passed him and won. After that I nearly killed myself inside because I was very hard with myself in those days. And that was my first experience of *Stars,* and so we were second.

I crewed for Desbarges in the European championship later on and we had a sail made from a French sailcoth, which was at that time very elastic, and we started with the two first places. The first race we won by speed and tactics, but the leach became more and more open, especially when the wind became stronger and stronger. So, in the second race, we were lying only third when the two first boats came across on starboard and one tacked and the other boat on port tack tacked too late, so their rigging tangled. Then the first one's mast broke and I told Albert, "Now we are second", and then the second mast broke, and so I said, "Now we are first." So we started with two first places but the wind became too strong in later races and we finished second, but that was mainly because we had not enough speed and this was because we were stupid enough to use the sails we made ourselves. We did not know enough about *Star-boat* sails.

Later that summer I went to Cowes with the old *5-0-5* to take part in some racing in Cowes Week, and when I came to England to try to get over to the Isle of Wight they told me in the first place I went to at Portsmouth that I could come over in August or September. I said, "Couldn't you help me because I have come all the way from Denmark and I am going to take part in a race". But nobody could help me.

Then I telephoned the club in Cowes, and I talked with the Secretary and I said I was a *5-0-5* sailor going to take part in the British Championships, and then the Secretary said, "Are you sailing a *5·5*?" "No", I said, "a *5-0-5*", and then I realized that he didn't know what a *5-0-5* was at all, and then I said, "It's a dinghy". "Oh, we have no dinghies here", and so I said, "If I said that I was coming from Denmark and taking part in racing in Cowes Week, would you say that you couldn't help me at all?" "No, I am sorry, I can't help you". When you are a young man coming from a foreign country, you feel that they will make you welcome, but later when I understood what this English yacht club was, then I understood it better.

So then I went to Southampton, but still I couldn't get over. Then I said, "O.K. Let us go to the shore at the closest point and see if I can sail over"; but I realized it was too far and what should I do with Anne and little Pia, who was three years old? But there we found a *Merlin-Rocket* sailor whose son was sailing over, and he said, "Come with me to the ferry and I will help you", and he spoke to the Captain telling the story, and in that way I got over. When I got to Cowes and met the other *5-0-5* sailors, the whole atmosphere was different.

I came in a small truck, and I parked it on the Saunders-Roe slipway and I put a tent over the top of the truck and that was where we lived. We sometimes moved to another place in the Isle of Wight and slept there.

Jasper Blackall

Jasper Blackall was crewing for me—I met Jasper when he won the Bronze Medal in Melbourne in the *Sharpie* class—and he was really such a charming fellow to sail with and we had a lot of fun. The most fun we had was with the trapeze belt. His was not strong enough to hold him, and he kept falling in the water, but when everything was strong enough to hold him, then we went like a bomb and we won.

Jasper had never been sailing with a spinnaker before. He came from the *12-square-metre Sharpie* class where there is no spinnaker and once we had 178 knots on this one, so at last I told him to take it down and we sailed without the spinnaker. But never mind—we were so much faster upwind that, even though we lost so much with no spinnaker, we came up again. Jasper's weight was fantastic when he

97

got it out, and when the wind was strong enough to keep him there.

But I saw an article on Cowes Week, which I remember, because it was quite amusing to see how an Englishman looked at my sailing. He was describing how we bore away round the mark and I hoisted the spinnaker and at the same time I took both sheets because Jasper was

From the left: Stewart Morris, Gold Medallist 1948, Jasper Blackall, Bronze Medallist 1956, Paul, Charles Currey, Silver Medallist 1952.

never able to get any routine with the spinnaker and so I did everything myself, and he had only to put the pole out.

The reporter said that I had the two sheets and the halliard, and the tiller between my legs and then I lost my trousers! I had enough to do, but he said that even then I had time to turn round to see where the others were. But he said something which I didn't realize that, even without this handicap, when the boat following put up its spinnaker it fell in and it was a long time before it caught the wind, but when we had hoisted our spinnaker it took the wind immediately and stayed there all the time and never collapsed. That was what the reporter said, but I had my eyes on my spinnaker and I couldn't see what was going on behind me; but it is quite nice when people say when a boat is handled right.

"... a ship came and we all had to stop ..."

I have heard so many people telling me, people who have sailed in Cowes and also local people, that Cowes is an awful place to sail but we liked going there. From my experience of Cowes Week that year I couldn't see why they said it was so awful. I liked the choppy waves and the tide which makes a special type of sea and I really found you need seamanship to sail there, and it was wonderful.

Of course, we had special problems such as one race where we rounded a mark near the start, and then set the spinnaker to go across toward the other shore and, unfortunately, a ship came and we all had to stop.

99

**Cowes and
Lymington 1957**

And another time we were trying to cross the bow of a tug which was towing a line of three barges, and it was risky. But, of course, if we crossed its bow we would gain a lot because all the people just behind would have to stop, and wait for it to pass. In a way that's seamanship and it's fun and you have to use your wits. It's more important to enjoy yourself than to get the result.

After Cowes, I took the family and went to stay with Richard Creagh-Osborne at Lymington, and we had nearly a week before we should go to France and take part in the World Championships.

And while I was at Lymington, we had some *Finn* racing and there was a very, very strong wind. I will never forget that. Richard said that, under certain wind conditions, it blows so hard from the Needles, and I remember I was planing, with my feet under the planing toe-straps in the stern, and I received such a hard puff and at the same time the water took me so that I was flying out of the toe-straps. I still had the mainsheet, but it was so long that the boat went away well balanced for about, let us say, eight yards before it capsized, and I had never sailed in such a puff.

In those days I didn't have any money at all, because I had spent it all on boats and sailing, and so I had to sell Richard my jib to be able to get money enough for the air ferry. We couldn't get a passage on the normal ferry and we had to take the air ferry from Lydd Airport, and I remember it was a sensation that the truck with the *5-0-5* on the back went in too and the whole plane-load went to France.

I had used the last of my money in a big supermarket in Southampton, and we filled up several trolleys and baskets with tins of food. I knew it would be too expensive in France. But then we had to get a hair cut, and Richard and I went across the road to a hairdresser's shop. I asked the hairdresser to give me short hair and afterwards I

Paul in 1956, nearing the end of his long-hair era.

saw it in the mirror and it was not short at all. So then I said, "You must take off more", and I understood he got a certain amount of money for one hair cut and he couldn't ask for more even if he did it once more. So he became angry and cut it so short that I looked like a prisoner-of-war. And that was how I changed my hair style from long hair to short. We laughed and said I could now sail faster, because it could not catch the wind so much.

When we got to France the carburettor on the truck fell off all the time, so I went into a place where there were some nails and I took four big ones. I took the screws out, put the four nails in and bent them over. It kept the carburettor on the motor and in that condition I sold the truck later.

I first went to Paris to pick up Pierre Poullain. I told him that the mast on the boat was so awful and with Pierre's light weight we could never go fast. So he fixed that we borrowed the good mast that we had the year before. But we were lucky we got strong winds so that we very rarely had to use the spinnaker because Pierre was a *Finn* sailor at that time, and he had no experience with a spinnaker at all. but we won all the races except one, and so won the Championship.

Later, the boat builder Lanaverre asked me if I would like a new *5-0-5*, and when I said, "Yes, if you would like my old one, I would like a new one", he said, "O.K.", and so I said, "Thank you very much".

101

Pierre Poullain

This was good for me because the next year in the World Championship there was no wind, but now I had a boat on minimum weight, so I won that World Championship too with Pierre.

We had a lot of fun, and I used to say that my hardest competitor was Pierre because in one race we were coming from behind and got to number two and then if we could make a perfect gybe we would pass Jacques Lebrun and be first in that race. So I said to Pierre, "Take hold of the kicking strap and you must not miss this gybe". He was so scared to miss it that he used all his strength to take the boom from one side to the other and he continued with it out into the water. I had to tack back to pick him up and I said, "It is more important that you stay here!" Two boats had passed us so we had to try to catch up again and then I remember on the last short upwind beat we broke something so I held the mainsail in with only one rope from the middle of the boom.

When I sailed with Pierre we used to speak together in English. I remember we were talking in a café and a British *Finn* sailor asked what language we were speaking. We said, "It is English. Don't you understand it? Where do you come from?" And he said he came from Oxford and Pierre answered, "Oh now I see why you don't understand us. We are from Cambridge!"

But sometimes things started to happen in a race too fast and I didn't know the French and I couldn't think of the English fast enough. Then I had to use the paddle on Pierre and he always understood that!

"... he always understood the paddle ..."

102

Paul, at the start of his short-haired, low-windage era, regards one of his bailers pensively.

Paul recalls that his Danish friend Aage Birch had the first *Dragon* sails that he ever made. It was in 1957 which was the year that the Queen of England visited Denmark. The Royal Yacht *Britannia* came and brought a number of British *Dragons* with her on the deck and one of these was the old boat *Bluebottle* which belonged to The Queen and Prince Philip and which had won a Bronze Medal at the Melbourne Olympics when skippered by Graham Mann.

Aage had built a beautiful new *Dragon* and now Paul takes up the story of the time when he was crewing him in the international series.

Paul. There were only three races and I remember the first race. It was a very light wind in the beginning and very flukey and we were at this time under spinnaker. We were not fast close reaching with the spinnaker because our spinnaker was too baggy at the top and there we learnt how important it was to make a spinnaker as flat in the top as possible. The old idea with the spinnaker was that it should lift the bow of the boat but this was the first spinnaker we ever made and we now learnt that it had to be flat when we were reaching. The flat spinnaker was much better than a baggy one.

We had the wind absolutely from behind when we came to the mark and the leading boats had no wind. There was a group of boats at the mark and so we kept our spinnaker up and continued down past them. We had to turn the mark to starboard but we went to the lee side of the whole group of boats still with the spinnaker up until we had passed them all and then at last we took the spinnaker down and pointed up and were leading. I like to tell this story because that was a really marvellous tactic. Other boats would have taken the spinnaker down and would have waited until it was time to turn the mark, but there were so many boats at the mark at that time that we would never have had a chance to pass close to the mark. There was only one way and that was to go to the lee side, but the important thing there was that we kept the spinnaker set even after we had passed the mark and not until we had passed them all on their lee side we took it down and luffed up and got a clear wind.

After that we went on to the port side of the course but over on our starboard side we could see that the clouds were very black. Bad weather was coming from a right angle to our course. So we tacked and alone we went up to starboard and we got the wind. There everything went as we had planned. It was not luck. We really went out to the side because we were sure we would have the wind first. It was the first race and we won it by a minute or two. The best of the other boats dropped down to about tenth and I think that we were second in the next two races.

Ole Berntsen's *Tip* was the winner of both the other races. He had the same speed upwind but with the spinnaker on close reaching he was faster. We lost ground there and we were not fast enough to take him on that point of sailing.

We learnt something else here about genoas. I remember that Strit Johansen made two genoas, one for medium and one for heavy weather and we first put up the medium one and we didn't think that the boat was going. It was not pointing. Then we took it down and put up the other one and at once the tiller became very light.

The next day Strit changed the medium one for an even heavier one and we found that the heavier one was again the best one. The lighter one was too baggy at the luff. So in all three races we changed the shape of the genoa but this really proved that even as a sailmaker you never know exactly what is the best shape. It was our first *Dragon* sail and we had to try many things because at that time we were not clever enough to tell when you cut it on the floor what will be the shape after the wind pressure had pushed it here and there.

Today we know more about it but still different water and different wind have to have different sails and we can only see by trial what sail is the fastest. No one is clever enough to tell when he sees it what sail is the fastest. You have to try it in a race. After this regatta in 1957 we did know something!

Six —————————————————————

Racing—1958 to 1962

Dragon Gold Cup
Marstrand, 1958

Paul. In 1958 I sailed with Aage Birch in his new boat in the Dragon
Gold Cup at Marstrand in Sweden. In this series Sorrentino of Italy had
the fastest boat on the course. We were about the next fastest. In the
last race Sorrentino went out on port in the last beat and we continued
on starboard. In that race if we finished ahead of Sorrentino we would
win the Gold Cup and if he was ahead then he would win. It was pure
luck who would win because the wind was so flukey that no one could
plan anything.

When we met on crossing tacks sometimes he was steering under
our stern and sometimes we were steering under his, and so it was pure
chance what would happen in the end. The result was that he came in
just ahead of us.

When things go like that and it is luck who would win then we
know that and we don't have to be disappointed. I liked that race but
if we had done any tactical mistake then we would have been angry
with ourselves. But not there. There was not that sort of feeling—only
pleasure.

I remember in the third race it was blowing like hell. We came to
the start one hour late because of the wind. Aage had not put on any
fittings for a working jib on the boat and we said how can we possibly
carry the genoa today. The wind speed was 21 metres per second
(42 knots) during the race and all the other Dragons set their working
jibs and when we were going out of the harbour I remember Ole
Berntsen called out to us, "Oh no! that will not work this time." But
there was nothing else we could do and so we went out.

We were starting on a dead run and we had the spinnaker pole on
the genoa. It was the old course that they had at Marstrand. It was
blowing so hard that only one boat, sailed by Torkild Warrer, put up a

Danish Dragon *sailor Ole Berntsen won the Silver Medal at Melbourne and the Gold Medal at Tokyo.*

Marstrand 1958

spinnaker but immediately, "Bang", there were only three leaches left with no sail in between them.

Aage. We came to the lee mark first with a big group just behind and there was a lot of banging and crashing. We started up the beat and were looking at the mast and saw we had sheeted in the mainsail too hard. So you took the main sheet in your hand and only looked at the mast all the time. We pulled in the genoa and were sailing on the genoa and a tiny piece of the mainsail leach—just enough to keep the boat in balance. I think that was the day when we learnt that whatever happened you can keep a genoa up and it will always be better than setting the working jib.

107

A typical Elvström start. Here he is several lengths clear of the field only a few seconds after the start of one of the races of the 1959 Finn Gold Cup.

Hard wind racing

Paul. We beat all the other *Dragons* so easily that day and afterwards no one put fittings on for working jibs any more. It showed that you shall never have another headsail than a genoa on a *Dragon* — never mind how much it blows.

There we were again two helmsmen in the boat and it worked perfectly. We had no arguments because if we had I would have remembered it.

Snipe World Championships 1959

The *Snipe* is the world's largest class and there is very good racing in *Snipes* in all parts of the world. Therefore I had always wanted to win this World Championship which is held every two years.

I had raced in this series in 1955 when it was in Santander in Spain but I had trouble with the boat which they lent me and I could not win. Mario Capio of Italy was the winner there.

I still wanted to win in this class and so I told my friend Strit Johansen that we would go to the 1959 World Championships in Porto Alegre, Brazil, but first I had to get selected. So I entered the Danish selection races with a young boy Ib Anderson, as crew and we won — from a fleet of 30 boats.

The Danish Sports Federation sent us but there was one member of the Committee who thought that it was a waste to send a crew all that way and so I was very nervous that I had to win.

At this time my temperament was very bad and each year I had more trouble. I felt that I had to win because everyone expected me to and I was scared of losing even a small race. I had so much nerves during these races that I became ill and in one race I was running on port gybe alongside the Duke of Arion who was on starboard and I luffed him. Of course he protested and I was disqualified.

At the protest discussion all I could do was say that I was sorry but I was ill. I have *never* done that before. I had so much nerves that I thought I was on starboard when I was on port.

110

*Snipes at
Porto Alegre
Brazil*

I have spoken later in the book about the boats which we used and how my mast broke in the training races. Then we got a new mast and it was more soft and the boat went very fast. The wind was medium in the World Championship races but one race was not finished and the last was cancelled. Therefore we only had four races and so we had to count all the points. We had two wins and a second and a disqualified but we still won so you can see we were much faster than the others.

It was at these races that I took the decision not to race any more because of my nerves. I said I would only go to the Olympics in Naples and then—finish!

European
One-man boat
Championships

I went to the European Championships in the *Finn* in 1960. It was on a small lake near Ostend and I was sailing very well but before the last race the situation was that Yves-Louis Pinaud of France could beat me if he won the race and I was below number three. Therefore my tactic was to cover him to keep him back. The tactic worked and so I won but Pinaud was so angry that he would not speak to me again. He said that it was not fair to use the rules like that but I said to him that we have to sail to what the rules say and they say you can cover a boat behind and so I had to do it to win.

I had trained especially to lose weight because we knew that there would be light winds in Naples for the Olympics and so I had lost four and a half kilos. We found that we really had quite light winds and when I got my boat I saw that I had a very soft mast and boom and such a flat sail that I had no speed at all.

At this Olympics we only had one mast and boom and we were not allowed to tune anything and so there was a lot of luck what speed we could get. There was only one thing to do and that was to hope they would break and then I could get some others because nothing could have been worse than the ones that I had.

111

I went out and sailed hard and one day we had a very strong wind from the sea. Even then I could not break them though, I was very hard with the boat, because they were like rubber but this wind must have weakened the boom because later I was sailing quietly and it broke.

I went to the jury for another boom but they asked me many questions how it broke and so on. They did not want to give me another boom because they said that everyone would be breaking their booms. I didn't say a word but I was thinking, "You have no need to worry. I tried so hard and I couldn't break it!"

Then they said I could have another boom and there were only two spare. They were discussing which one to give me but I told Bjorg Schwarz, "Come on, we will both go in together and take the stiff one." I thought they would stop us but we got the boom.

Then my speed was a little better and I won the first race. In the second race I found Pinaud number two just ahead of me in third place, and he started to cover me. We were sailing slower and slower and I was trying to sail through his lee when there was a very big windshift and we had to tack but this put me right behind him again.

I tried again and then I started to go through and at the moment that I was sure to pass him Pinaud became so angry that he stood up in his boat and was shouting and banging and making a lot of noise. I think he finished number seven and I was fifth.

But after the race Pinaud came up to me and shook hands and said, "Let us forget about our argument" and since then we have always been good friends.

In another race I was disqualified by the jury for starting too early but I was sure that I was right. I had gone to the port end of the line and they had no jury boat there. They only were looking from the Committee boat at the other end. I was too early and Dan Mackenzie of Kenya and Louis Scheiss of Switzerland were also over the line to windward of me. I bore away and tacked to the lee side of the line and then started on port tack. Mackenzie and Schiess and also Ian Bruce of Canada and Per Jordebakke of Norway all came to the protest discussion to tell them I was right. That was an example of how racing should be. Even in the Olympic Games these sailors came to say this so that their hardest competitor should not be disqualified unfairly.

In the night before the sixth race I became very ill. It was a combination of my nerves and the food that I was not used to. I was completely unconscious and Anne had to drag me on the floor to my bed. In the morning I felt awful but I had to go out and then as the

It is hard to believe from this happy picture, taken at Naples, that the actual racing was such a trial to Paul that he was to give up for almost three years.

gun tired I felt better. All went well and I won the race. Afterwards I knew I had won the Gold Medal but I was feeling so ill and my nerves were so bad that I could not start in the last race.

5·5-metres

1. United States, George O'Day   2, 4, 1, 3, 1, 7, 1   6900
2. Denmark, W. E. Berntsen   1, 5, 5, 1, 10, 8, 2   5678.
3. Switzerland, H. Copponex   3, 1, 4, 5, 8, 3, 13   5122.
4. Argentine, R. Sieburger.
5. Sweden, B. Sjosten.
6. Great Britain, Robin Aisher.
7. Norway, Finn Ferner.
8. Bahamas, Bobby Symonette.
9. Germany, H. Scholl.
10. Australia, Jock Sturrock.
11. Italy, P. Reggio.
12. Bermuda, A. Darrell.
13. Spain, E. Bertrand.
14. U.S.S.R., V. Gorlov.
15. Finland, P. Tallberg.
16. Portugal, D. Bello.
17. Austria, G. Kochert.
18. France, Jaques Lebrun.

Dragons

1. Greece, Crown Prince
   Constantine   10, 3, 3, 1, 4, 2, 4   6733.
2. Argentine, C. J. A. Salas   15, 1, 2, 5, 2, D, 10   5715.
3. Italy, A. Cosentino   5, 2, 1, 2, 11, 14, D   5704.
4. Norway, O. Christensen.
5. Canada, S. McDonald.
6. Denmark, Aage Birch.
7. Great Britain, G. Mann.
8. Germany, H. Ravenborg.
9. Portugal, C. F. J. Ferreira.
10. United States, E. Walet.
11. Australia, H. Brooke.
12. Eire, A. J. Mooney.
13. Holland, W. van Duyl.
14. France, Jean Peytel.
15. Bermuda, Brownlow Eve.
16. U.S.S.R., E. Stayson.
17. Finland, R. Nyman.
18. Bahamas, G. Kelly.
19. Uruguay, H. Garcia.
20. Sweden, B. Palmquist.
21. Switzerland, R. Thorens.
22. Japan, M. Ishii.
23. Philippines, F. Prysler.
24. Monaco, J. Socca.
25. Singapore, E. Holiday.
26. Indonesia, A. Danudirdjo.
27. Spain, S. Pi.

Stars

1. U.S.S.R., Timir Pinegin   1, 2, 1, 1, 3, 5, 5   7619
2. Portugal, M. Quina   3, 3, 8, 2, 5, 1, 3   6665.
3. United States, William Parks   9, 7, 4, 3, 2, 4, 1   6269.
4. Italy, A. Straulino.
5. Switzerland, H. Bryner.
6. Bahamas, Durward Knowles.
7. Germany, Bruno Splieth.
8. Jugoslavia, M. Fafangel.
9. Brazil, J. Pontual.
10. Sweden, S. Carlsson.
11. France, G. Pisani.
12. Hungary, I. Telegdi.
13. Cuba, J. de Cardenas.
14. Finland, F. A. Ehrstrom.
15. Austria, H. Musil.
16. Mexico, C. Branif.
17. Argentine, R. Mieres.
18. Austria, R. French.
19. Thailand, Prince Bira.
20. Greece, N. Vlagalis.
21. Venezuela, D. Camejo.
22. Spain, J. A. Ocejo.
23. Canada, W. Burgess.
24. Great Britain, Roy Mitchell.
25. Malta, P. Ripard.
26. Japan, M. Yamada.

Flying Dutchman	1. Norway, P. Lunde and B. Bergvall	2, 2, 10, 5, 1, 3, 10 6774.
	2. Denmark, H. Fogh and O. Petersen	7, 18, 1, 8, 5, 1, 13 5991.
	3. Germany, R. Mulka and I. von Bredow	3, 10, 13, 2, D, 6, 1 5882

4. Rhodesia, A. Butler and C. Bevan
5. Holland, G. Verhagen and G. Lautenschutz
6. U.S.S.R., A. Shelkolnikov and V. Pilchin
7. Great Britain, Slotty Dawes and James Ramus
8. New Zealand, M. Rae and R. Watson
9. Switzerland, P. Siegenthaler and M. Buzzi
10. Eire, Johnny Hooper and C. Gray
11. Italy, Mario Capio and T. Pizzorno
12. Spain, J. A. Allende and G. Laiseca
13. Hungary, I. Holenyi and A. Molnar
14. France, J. C. Cornu and D. Gouffier

15. South Africa, Helmut Stauch and R. Standing
16. Bermuda, de F. Trimingham and R. Divall.
17. Austria, C. Autereid.
18. Kenya, A. Bentley-Buckle.
19. Australia, Rolly Tasker.
20. United States, Harry Sindle.
21. Belgium, J. de Brouwere.
22. Canada, Pierre des Jardines.
23. Greece, C. Limberakis.
24. Sweden, C. Vinge.
25. Bahamas, G. Lightbourn.
26. Brazil, R. W. Edgard.
27. Portugal, C. Braga.
28. Indonesia, E. S. Lie.
29. Burma, K. P. Gyi.
30. West Indies, R. Bennett.
31. Lebanon, Fred Zebouni.

Finn Monotypes	1. Denmark, Paul Elvström	1, 5, 1, 2, 5, 1, N/S 8171.
	2. U.S.S.R., A. Chuchelov	7, 1, 2, 10, 17, 2, 8 6520.
	3. Belgium, Andre Nelis	2, 2, 12, 24, 3, 15, 4 5934.

4. Australia, Ron Jenyns
5. Brazil, Reinaldo Conrad
6. New Zealand, R. Roberts
7. Canada, Ian Bruce
8. Bahamas, Kenneth Albury
9. France, Y. L. Pinaud
10. Jugoslavia, T. Pivcevic
11. United States, Peter Barrett
12. Great Britain, Vernon Stratton
13. Norway, Per Jordebakke
14. Italy, Bruno Trani
15. Portugal, H. de Oliviera
16. Finland, Youko Valli.
17. Austria, Peter Furst.
18. Eire, J. Somers Payne.
19. Argentine, Ricardo Boneo.

20. Germany, Hans Kammerer.
21. Spain, The Duke of Arion.
22. Greece, Joannis Kariofillis.
23. Japan, Yasuo Hozumi.
24. Holland, Hans Sleezwijk.
25. Hungary, K. Tolnai.
26. Switzerland, Louis Scheiss.
27. Turkey, Erzin Demir.
28. Sweden, Goeran Andersson.
29. Kenya, Dan Mackenzie.
30. Burma, Maung Maung Lwin.
31. Morocco, El Mostapha Haddad.
32. Bermuda, Brownlow Gray.
33. South Africa, G. Burn-Wood.
34. Malta, Alfred Borda.
35. Lebanon, P. Arbaji.

In 1959 when he was at Porto Alegre Paul decided to give up racing after the 1960 Olympics. The nervous build-up over the years finally became too great to bear. In actual fact he did race seriously once more but that was as crew to Hans Fogh in the 1962 *Flying Dutchman* World Championships described later. Apart from this he was mostly just watching through his binoculars the races taking place on the perfect arena laid out before his window at Hellerup.

The Olympic Course was only 500 yards or so away, whilst the Courses for the evening races which were held almost daily throughout the summer passed close in front of him and the boats and crews were in full view. Not only that, the power-boat was ready for instant use if something appeared which excited his curiosity and demanded closer inspection.

But Paul certainly did not stop sailing. He was constantly on the water tuning boats and testing sails and he also took part in friendly races in many places. He went to Tokyo three years running at the request of Mr. Ozawa who was Vice-President of the Japan Yachting Association and who was responsible for organizing the whole of the Olympic Yachting including the construction of the vast yacht harbour at Enoshima.

The Japanese held trial races in Sagami Bay to test the arrangements and I took part in those of 1963 together with Paul, when we had almost no wind for the whole period. Fortunately in the following year the wind was quite good and from quite another direction, and so all the races were completed.

My job in 1963 was to measure the *Finns* and to work out the arrangements, which were quite new to this regatta, in which the organizers were going to give each competitor two masts and booms and a limited amount of spare gear and then let them tune their allotted boats using only this equipment and nothing more.

Paul and I had discussed this problem of the tuning of the Olympic *Finns* in previous regattas and I had tried to get something done about it ever since 1956. Now, at last, the Japanese were receptive to the idea and so I was able, as Technical Chairman of the *Finn* class to get the arrangements started.

The competitors were most ingenious in their use of the equipment. One made a clew outhaul out of half of his main halyard wire but we could not discover what he had used to serve the splices. Eventually he told us that he had taken the outer cover off the shock cord which pulled the centreboard down and had made some twine out of these strands of cotton. Another man sliced a piece off his tiller to make a wedge for his boom mortice and at the same time this allowed him to lift his tiller as he was used to doing on his own boat.

116

Paul spent much of his time studying racing from his speed boat.

The result was that the sailors were, for the first time in an Olympic series, able to use the knowledge they had won from their experiences in international racing, and tune their boats to suit their own weights. The idea was successful and was used again in Mexico in 68.

There is little doubt that Paul's success in the Olympic Games was due in some part to his great strength and higher than average weight. At Naples due to mainly lightish winds, his weight was not so necessary and so we can see that in all facets of racing skill he was paramount at that time because he still won convincingly.

Hans Fogh

Hans Fogh was working in the family flower growing business near Copenhagen and met Paul as a result of Hans' father buying the second *Pirat* class sail that Paul ever made. As we shall see it was because of this chance event that Paul's infant sail loft received a tremendous boost which more than anything put it on the road to world wide success.

Hans Fogh's racing success and his determination to win eventu-

117

ally led him to abandon the family business and to join Paul in his sail
loft. He became Paul's chief sail cutter and then production manager.
He moved with the loft from Hellerup to Rungsted and from Rungsted
to the splendid new premises at Kokkedal about half way between
Copenhagen and Helsingor.

Hans was probably the "hardest trier" of all the Danish international
sailors. Even Paul whose energy and determination are legendary in this
department, was surprised and even astonished at Hans' single-minded
devotion to the business of gaining international honours.

Hans started in the *Pirat* class, one of the biggest classes in and
around Germany. The *Pirat* is a rather heavy hard-chine boat—flat and
rather narrow—rather like a small international *Sharpie* and carries a
low aspect sloop rig. Incidentally, the *O.K.* dinghy was designed by the
Danish designer, Knud Olsen, around the *Pirat* mainsail. The *O.K.* was
intended as a simple, exciting boat for the children of older *Pirat*
sailors. It was very cheap, since it could use cast-off *Pirat* mainsails.
The *O.K.* was not intended as a *Finn* trainer as is so often thought
nowadays.

Later, Hans moved into the *Flying Dutchman* class in partnership
with a young civil engineer, Ole Gunnar Petersen, but since they had
almost the only *Flying Dutchman* in Denmark, they used to train in
Finns on the Sound from Hellerup Sailing Club.

Hans had great success in both these international classes, just
failing to win the *Finn* Gold Cup more than once, and gaining a Silver
Medal in the *Flying Dutchman* class at Naples in 1960. He went on to
win the World Championship in 1962 and was fourth in the Olympics at
Tokyo. He also sailed at Acapulco, but had to return home in the middle
of the series, when his father died suddenly.

The following conversation was recorded only a few days before
he left Denmark with his family for good, to set up his own Elvström
sail loft in Toronto, Canada:

Paul. The first time that I met Hans was because of the second *Pirat*
sail we ever made. His father bought it for him. He got it just before a
race in *Pirats* in 1955.
Hans. Yes. I was going to a big regatta and we had to sail there because
we had no trailer at that time. So we went there using my old sail and
then my father said, "Here is another sail for you to try". It was in a
green bag which was different from all the others. This was, of course,

the new Elvström sail in the green bag which was to become so well
known.

    We were in the "B" class. There were so many they had to
divide the fleet. There were about twenty boats in "B", and sixty to
seventy in the "A" class. They did not know me, and I did not know the
class and so of course we had to start from the bottom. We won that
race very easily and we got the third best time overall of "A" or "B"
boats. So probably we would have finished in the first five had we been
in the "A" class.

Paul. What you did over there gave Strit Johansen and me a big push in
sail making because, when a beginner really goes fast with a new sail,
everybody is sure that it is the sail and not the sailor! This success made
nearly all the very big *Pirat* class come and get their sails from me.

Hans. We won the first race by three or four minutes. In the second
race we were so far ahead that my father asked what was wrong. Did
we touch a mark? We said that we had just finished, and he asked
where the others were. We said they were coming. We really got a speed
in that race!

Paul. The main story here was in 1962 where you and I went to
Florida to take part in the World Championship of the *Flying Dutchman*
class. We had a lot of practice before this. You bought a new German
Flying Dutchman and I wanted to try using only one trapeze wire. We
tried to do it in such a way that I was flying over round the bow when
we tacked, but we had to give up very early because it was too
dangerous and my feet went into the genoa sheets and it gave so many
troubles.

Hans. Once we made a perfect tack. You went to the bow and when we
passed head-to-wind you went out on the trapeze on the other side,
but it was too slow. In a trapeze boat you have to tack fast like a *Finn*.
But it happened once and if we had been in training I think that it
could have been done. It would have been very, very difficult and we
had no time to perfect it.

Paul. With that boat we went to Ski-Yachting in January in Cannes,
and the World Championship was in March.

    At the Ski-Yachting regatta we were to check that the speed was
O.K. and we found it very slow. So we went home and took the old
Flying Dutchman that you won the Silver Medal with in Naples and
that boat we shipped to Florida. In one or another way it happened that
the boat was still in the docks at New York when we arrived, and so we
flew it down to Miami and picked it up at the airport. But we found there

were some holes in the hull where they had dropped it, and we had to fix these. So finally we were only able to sail on the day before the racing started.

Hans. Before this during the winter we did some experiments with Paul which were a very great help. When I was sailing with Ole Gunnar Petersen, my crew from the Olympic Games in Rome, we sometimes had difficulty when running with the spinnaker set, because we often capsized and this is a very bad mistake. But Paul taught me to be able to sail with the spinnaker in heavy weather. It really happened one day in January when it was blowing about Force 6 or 7 from the coast. We went out to about the middle of the Sound reaching and running with the spinnaker, which I will never forget because I was so frightened of capsizing. At this time of the year there was nobody on the water, and it is quite cold and nearly dark. Every time I became afraid Paul make me nearly quiet again because he showed me that the way to steer a spinnaker if you know how to do it is just as easy as handling a rudder. I mean that you can steer the boat just like using a rudder.

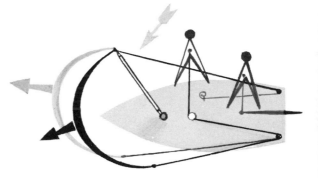

You can steer a spinnaker as easily as a rudder. In hard winds you can ease and haul the sheet and you can see from the drawing that you can correct too much heeling to windward or to leeward in this way.

Paul. What I did was to cleat the spinnaker pole guy on the windward side, and I had the lee sheet in one hand and each time the boat was heeling to windward, I said to Hans, "Look! I pull in", and the boat came upright! In that way Hans became used to it and became quiet. I remember it got very dark but I wanted Hans to be sure that when we handled the spinnaker in that way we could never capsize. So it was not until Hans absolutely trusted me that we went in and it was absolutely dark when we were beating in to the shore.

Hans. We were sailing as much as possible and another time we went out also when it was nearly dark. But the funny thing there was

120

Paul and his circle trained hard. Here Bjorg Schwarz wends his way through the ice floes to come ashore after training.

that there was no ice on the water when we went out but as we came to sail in we had to go through ice which had formed whilst we were out. It was just two or three hours later. So you can see that we trained hard! *Paul.* After this very good preparation we went to Florida with the old boat — D4. We went out to test our speed against the others and realized that we were not fast.

We did not know what to do, but next day we started and I can only remember the finish of that race. It was in a very light wind. We seemed to have about the same speed as everyone in that wind, and we thought we were O.K. Adrian Jardine of England was leading and we were just behind. Just before we reached the finishing line the wind suddenly came quite strong and we still had about the same speed as Jardine. We had a close-reaching wind and so we were planing but one boat was coming up from behind like a rocket. It was Rolly Tasker from Australia, and he was only half a boat's length behind at the finish. So the finish line saved us and we kept the second place, but then we knew how really slow we were.

There was something special I remember in the second race. We were leading — if we could say that anyone was leading, because we were all spread out — but Jardine was fifty yards to leeward and I saw a big flat patch ahead and to windward. If we had continued we

121

would have gone into this dead hole so we tacked immediately and when we came on the left side of this hole we tacked again. Jardine from England continued into the hole and I think he finished well down the fleet and we finished second again.

When Jardine came into the shore he said that he had been absolutely blind. He realized when he came into that flat patch that he should have tacked before and he was wondering when we tacked if he should follow us, but it was too late. It is a big advantage to be able to see things before they happen.

It is a good rule that what you *can* see, you *must* see. All the things which you cannot foresee — never mind beforehand or afterwards. Do not think of them any more.

There was a very windy race and we were still not the fastest boat. I was using the low trapeze position and I think I had 25 kilos of water in my clothing. I had the feeling when I first went out on the trapeze that because I first had to drop down and then go out that I would break the whole boat, I was so heavy. We had no winch. We had only the ratchet blocks on the lee deck. Also the old type of polypropylene genoa sheets and I remember how hard it was on the hands.

Hans. To pull in the genoa properly you had to take a turn round the trapeze hook and then straighten your legs. Otherwise you couldn't get it in because of the hard wind.

Paul. That race the fastest boat didn't make the best use of the wind shifts and that was the main reason that we won. We also went the way that gave us the closest heading to the mark. But on the second beat we got a heading shift where we both fell back into the water. If the wind shift had been five degrees more we would have capsized to windward. It was such a squally wind. I went into the water because I was in the trapeze and you went in also to try to keep the boat up.

Hans. The New Zealanders were to leeward and close to us and they capsized and you asked where they were. I told you and so you laughed, but they nearly were able to laugh at us because we were so nearly capsized too. I came out of the toe straps and jumped into the water to put a hand underneath the boat to try to stop it capsizing. Then I had to climb up into the boat again because we just had to win this race.

Paul. Yes, but then the wind came back and pushed us up again. But I am sure that you went into the water because that was the fastest way to right the boat rather than trying to climb across to the other side. I think that your reaction was that the fastest thing that you could do was to fall back into the water. Like in the *Finn* that quite often happens

122

when the wind is very shifty. You have your whole body in the water and you just have to wait.

We won that race and I had the feeling that we were handling our boat much better than everyone else but we really had that boat tuned very badly and it was hard work for us. If our boat was tuned right then we would win by many minutes. So when we passed the line first we did not have a nice feeling. We were sad that our boat was so slow.

Hans. In that race we had the spinnaker up of course and I feel that this was where our training of three or four months before in the Sound in Denmark helped us. There were the Kraan brothers from Holland close to us and instead of keeping close to them and safe we gybed to pick up a good wind shift and went at least ten boat lengths ahead at the mark. Instead of being afraid to capsize on gybing we did not think about capsizing because we had done so much practice.

We gained ten boat lengths only by our technique and that was the only reason we won there. We did exactly what we would like to do to get there fastest. We were not scared of anything. We had one other strong wind race and I think we finished second.

We had three seconds and a first out of the first four races and most people thought we were sure winners but we knew how slow we really were. We knew we had to sail seven races here and we did not like that because Rolly Tasker from Australia had a wonderful speed. Luckily he did not make the best of the tactics.

Paul. Yes, if he had made the same tactics as we did he would have had seven first places.

The last race none of us will ever forget. I got a baby the night before and Anne phoned me to tell me. She couldn't understand why I was not so happy and why I was not talking about the baby. But it was because I only had the last race in my head. Nothing else.

It was so that if the Australian came first we had to be number five or higher to keep first place overall. We knew that he could easily win because his speed was so good, and we could easily be lower than fifth because ours was so bad. So the only tactic we could do was to cover him from the start and try to do all that we could so that together we became last and the one before last.

We worked out that we should always start on his lee side because, for example, if we started on starboard tack and we were on his lee side then we could stop his speed by pointing high.

So, five minutes before the start we were watching him all the time and we were very careful not to put ourselves in a place where we

123

couldn't keep him back. The only thing that we were afraid of was that he would go down to the lee mark and start on port tack because there it would make problems for us as his speed was so tremendous that we had to start in a way where we really would cover him.

When we were on his lee side and we were both on starboard tack and we were pinching and slowing his speed down we knew that neither of us could tack because of all the other starting boats. So we knew that in this way we could gain speed after that start by freeing off and if he tacked later then we would be well ahead and could tack and try to get a better speed by not pointing too high and then cover him again.

That was exactly what happened and he only first realized our plan after the gun. We tacked about five times and we were last and second to last and then, during one tack onto port, my port genoa sheet made a knot so that I couldn't get the starboard genoa sheet in. There we lost him and had to say goodbye.

He eventually reached number six about half way through the race but could not get past the fifth boat and we stayed back in about number sixteen. We won the World Championship but Hans and I had such a bad feeling winning a World Championship with such a bad speed.

After the race I remember Rolly Tasker said to Hans and me that we were lucky. I must say that he was not absolutely right that we were lucky because if he had known how slow our boat really was he would have seen that it was so difficult to have won the World Championship. So it was not really fair to say that we were lucky. I remember he said, "Now I know what 'hard international tactics' means". I said, "Maybe" but this tactic was the only way we could win with such a slow speed. We had to do it. But it was not really hard international tactics because that means jumping into the other man's boat and pulling the mast down. That's hard international tactics. But I would not do that!

At that time it was not allowed in the rules to bear away to cover a boat who wanted to pass you on the lee side when going to windward. So we sailed a little freer than normal so that we were nearly breaking the rule but it was just on the borderline. The rules were very weak so that even if we had broken the rule he could have done nothing about it. But let us say that he could have proved that we had broken a rule but still nothing could hurt us in that race even if we had been disqualified. It was our throwout race. The rules were a little weak. The rule should have been worded so that he had a chance to win the World Championship and we had a chance to lose. In this case if we

broke the rule he still had no chance to win the World Championship.
He took his chance away and we kept our own World Championship
and the rule should have been so that we could have been
disqualified in all races by using that tactic. That would have been
more fair. But rules are rules and it is very difficult to make them fair.
But the rules were like that at that time and we took advantage of it.

That was my last international race and then I stopped, and for
three years after that I was not racing but I watched racing from power
boats.

Hans. My feeling was that in this World Championship it really was a
team effort and not just racing with a helmsman and his crew. The only
thing for me was to steer the boat right and to tack perfectly when
Paul said tack and I know Paul would make better tactics than anyone
else could. If I wanted to know what the others were doing Paul just
shouted to me and told me because my job was only to keep the boat at
the best speed possible through the water and I only looked at the flag
at the top of the mast and the luff of the sail. I didn't really see my
competitors in the whole race. It was complete team work.

A two-man boat must be sailed by two men. One man has his
job as tactician and the other man has to steer. It must also be the same
in a three-man boat and so on. No member of the crew must be on
board just for fun. They must all have their jobs otherwise you will
never get a good result.

Paul. You're right Hans. It was very good that we came on to this point
because a two-man, three-man or four-man boat really must have team
work to get the best speed. I can say that in the *Flying Dutchman* in
Florida I was able to concentrate on the tactics one hundred per cent
because I knew that Hans kept the tiller correctly. At the same time I
will say that if we were not in the best position in every start then
nobody else was better. We were always amongst the best in every
start.

It is wonderful to be a crew when you work hard. It must be awful
to have a stupid crew who makes bad mistakes and loses time and
then you have to work double so hard to win it back. There I must say
that it is the only time in my life that I have enjoyed crewing because
I am a better helmsman than the people I've crewed for, but not with
Hans. I could not have steered the boat better myself and therefore I
enjoyed it. This team work was the only reason that we won the
World Championship with that slow boat.

Hans. For me to have a crew like Paul was like being pushed hard over
the line. Paul could see exactly when we were on the line and the

126

moment when we could pull in the sheets and go full speed across the line at the last second. We were really flying at the starts every time and I think it was a big handicap for Tasker that we always were ahead of him at the start.

In the last race when he knew we were close to him from five minutes before the start he became so nervous that he made a very bad start. I think that he knew from the other five or six races that we were always ahead and he felt that it would also happen in the last race. He really gave up before the start.

That is an example of how the tactics can start before the start where you show people you are better than them. Then they get afraid of you and they don't think that they can beat you. It is a shock that can stop them from doing their best on the course right from the beginning.

Paul. We had another race I remember very clearly. In this race there was a light wind. We started at the lee end of the line and the wind was turning so we got more and more freed. So the boats who were in the right side of the course out to sea became farther and farther ahead of us and so we were down amongst the four last places. It was a triangle and on the next upwind leg we could easily lay the finishing line, but four of the leading boats were going too high because they were hoping to get more wind first. But what we did was to bear away so that we had a chance of getting some wind ahead of the leading boats which they could not get.

It is a theoretical idea and if the wind came from their side they would win but if it came from our side we had a chance. So what I would like to say here is that my basic tactic has always been when behind to put ourselves in a position where we did really have a chance to win. If we just followed the others there was no question but that we would stay down there. But we went down to leeward and the wind came from ahead of the leading boat. We got it at the same time as the leaders and so we came up to number seven, two places ahead of Tasker.

Before the finishing line I remember we were close to Rolly Tasker. Because of this I had the feeling that because of his complex about us he might do stupid things with a spinnaker. You remember he came up and then bore away and put up the spinnaker and he was finished. When you bear off in a *Flying Dutchman* you are dead.

He tried to hoist the spinnaker and this was very bad for him because he spoilt his speed more than he would have done by going on without his spinnaker.

127

There is another story I would like to pick up here because it has always been my idea never to give up whatever happens and so now we go to where you were sailing in the Olympic Games in Tokyo and you broke your boom and I think that because of your sailing here with me you knew that whatever happens you must never give up if there is the slightest chance of finishing. Here you broke your boom and you finished the race as number four after you had been leading by miles.

Hans. We had several minutes lead before going to the last mark and before then we had broken the halliard twice. First we broke it and the ball that keeps it into the halliard lock slipped through the slot and so then we had to tie up the halliard by the tail line which was spliced into the wire and we lashed it to the centreboard case.

Broken halliards

So we continued but the mainsail was not very well set but it did not matter—we had this enormous lead and we thought we could just keep ahead. But later on this halliard broke again where it was spliced into the wire. This time the rope broke because it was only a 4 mm. thin line for hoisting the mainsail before clipping it into the masthead lock. So we nearly lost the whole thing because the end of the wire went up through the mast but it stuck just before the gooseneck.

My crew, Ole, just saw the wire and he put his hand on it and stopped it there and then he tied it up and put a few knots round the gooseneck and then we continued again. I now thought that we were in good shape because surely nothing more can happen with that halliard! We still had a really good lead which we had gained because of our good team work and because of our training for hours and hours and we had become even better in strong winds.

Broken boom

Then, finally, we had this bad luck to break the boom and I really didn't know what to do. I only said that we must continue because we can still win this race. But the others came closer and closer and started to pass us and after the finishing line I realized what we should have done. We should have taken the spinnaker pole and put it inside the boom in such a way that we could have used the mainsail a little more effectively.

So maybe we could have won this race. It was only two-and-a-half minutes at the finish between the first and the fourth boat which was us.

Paul. If the wind had become stronger then it would have been all right. Because it would be almost an advantage that you had a free leach to the mainsail. What I like is that you are thinking what you should have done and so next time if it happens that your boom breaks you will know what to do immediately.

128

K. Hashimoto

Hans Fogh and Ole Petersen cross the finish line in an Olympic race at Tokyo,
after a multitude of accidents.

Seven

World Championship Years— 1966 and 1967

Starting racing
again

At Tokyo in '64 I didn't compete and was spare man because the Danish Olympic Committee thought that I should go there. They had the feeling something would be wrong if I wasn't there and so they asked me to be spare man but I didn't know what boat I was spare man for. But it was there that I got the interest in racing back. I felt that now I could compete in sailing without being nervous because when I was watching the competitors in Tokyo I realized how stupid it was to be nervous about competing in something I loved. So I had the feeling I would like to compete again and so later, after the IYRU meeting in London, I went to Paris to visit Pierre and he said, "Shouldn't we go to Adelaide in Australia and compete in the *5-0-5* World Championships because it is eight years since we won it last?". In 1958 we won the last time and I thought he was joking but I said, "O.K. But I have heard in Adelaide there are strong winds and so because of my experience in the trapeze, it is better that I take the trapeze". "Oh fine," said Pierre. I began to think it would be fun to go to Adelaide but Pierre couldn't understand that I would want to keep the tiller at the same time as the trapeze. He didn't understand me and thought I was going to crew for him but I am an honest person and so I said, "Pierre, I would never crew you because I don't like that idea. No I am helming and taking the trapeze too, so let us go through the rules to see if it is allowed". The rules said that only one man may stay on the trapeze and so Pierre telephoned the *5-0-5* Secretary to ask if we could enter. He said, yes, and so we bought a boat and sent it to Adelaide.

In London we met each other at the airport for the *5-0-5* class charter flight and I had in my hand an extension to the tiller extension

130

At the World Championship at Adelaide, Australia, Paul introduced the remarkable technique of steering from the trapeze with his crew in the normal position.

and when the other competitors who were travelling with us asked me what it was I said it was an extension to the tiller extension. So they laughed and didn't think about it again until they realized later it was not a joke.

During the Australian Championship races, which were before the
World Championships, I went out standing in trapeze and everything
worked fine.

I must say that Pierre's father died and so he had to leave Adelaide
before the first race ever started but I got a local young chap, Pip
Pearson, who crewed for me and he did very well.

We won the two first races and I remember the first was in very
light winds and we were on a close reach coming to the finish line from
the last mark. Cuneo of Australia, who was second in that race, had a
little fuller jib and for that reason, I think, he was gaining on me, and
he came closer and closer and tried to pass to windward. I worked
out that if he continued with his speed I could pass the commitee boat
on the wrong side and then gybe and go back and still win. But
suddenly, fifty yards before the finishing line, he bore off and hoisted
his spinnaker and, of course, I bore off immediately so he couldn't
succeed at all and I was sure to win. It was much easier like that than if
he had continued on my windward side; I say this because it is an
example of how I had calculated what to do when he came closer and
closer so that whatever he did he would never win that race.

The next race was in a very strong wind and I remember I stayed
on the trapeze with the tiller also. We had about twenty metres per
second (40 knots) which is very, very strong for a 5-0-5 and when we
were planing I stayed on the trapeze and twice the sea knocked me
down to the rudder. But I kept the boat in balance because Pip was
hanging normally in the toe straps. But that was the last time I stayed on
the trapeze with the tiller when planing on a 5-0-5 because that was
really hard work in such strong wind. Most people capsized or retired
but we never capsized and we managed to finish that race. The tanks
were very shiny and smooth and I was so tired mainly because everything was so slippery in the boat, but afterwards it was a nice feeling to
have been able to do that seamanship and finish the race.

In the last race it was a very close fight with John Cuneo and Jim
Hardy of Australia, and Larry Marks from England. We had to finish
first with Jim Hardy not higher than fourth and Cuneo sixth to win the
championship. I sailed well and was leading and I saw that Jim Hardy
was about number twenty-two. But he got a fantastic speed and he
came up faster and faster and I could do nothing. Finally he finished

second but I was so pleased that such a good competitor and such a
nice person could have beaten me. And it was also a nice feeling that
after eight years away from the 5-0-5 I could so nearly win the World
Championship and anyway, it would not have mattered if I had finished

number one, two, three or four, inside I was happy that I could still steer and sail a *5-0-5*. And we did that without training at all and with a crew I had never seen before. It is a pity I have not had time for *5-0-5* sailing since then. I hope I will be back one day because I still love that boat.

During the World Championship the Press in Australia was very good, and Colin Ryrie sent reports through the radio. There was a music programme and the music stopped when we turned each mark and Colin gave his radio report so that all Australia was every day following the World Championship of the *5-0-5s*. It became such a big

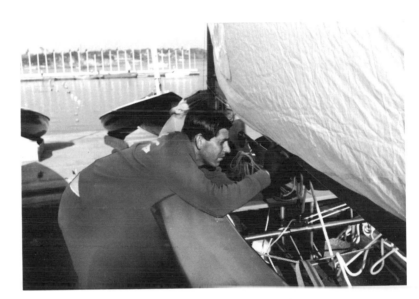

Olympic Finn *sailor, Colin Ryrie, is now running the Elvström sail loft in Sydney, Australia.*

success because the Australian just managed to win and, of course, that was a wonderful result for the Australian listeners. They told me that what Colin did on the radio was the best propaganda for yachting and I am sure such things help to get people out sailing.

Before I went to Adelaide I was a little stupid, but I decided as well as the *5-0-5* to compete in the World Championship in *5·5-metres* and in the *Star* World Championships after that. John Albrechtson, the Swedish *Star-boat* sailor, who had won the North American Championship that year, had three bets with me that I would not win all three championships. I really did it for fun and we were both laughing. Every bet was for one hundred Swedish crowns and when

I came back from Adelaide I gave him the money and said, "You have won but it was very close". But then I said to him. "But wait, I will get them back". Later that season when I won the 5·5-metres, he gave me the hundred Swedish crowns back but he said. "O.K. in the *Star* I will have them back". He wanted to beat me himself but he was not selected for Sweden so I bought his boat and he crewed for me. But then we won and so he gave me the one hundred Swedish crowns. That was really a joke.

A challenge

It was also really a joke how I came to race the 5·5-metre. In '66 I think it was, we should have the World Championships in Copenhagen and Willy Berntsen, who had come tenth in Tokyo, had bought a new one and so I asked him if I could borrow the old one for this championship and he said "Yes, do that". He said that I would never get that boat going, but that was really a challenge. I felt that I would like to prove that the sail shape and tuning was more important than the boat shape. I thought at that time that there wasn't so much difference between most of the boats but I was lucky that no design had really improved on this boat.

Puerto Rico and
a broken leg

But before this comes the big story. I was invited to take part in some races in Puerto Rico outside San Juan and the morning after I got there I went out to try the boat they had lent me. It was a *Finn* and I set off together with Ding Schoonmaker and immediately realized that the mast was too soft for the sail I had so I decided to go to the shore to get a stiffer mast. I sailed towards the beach and took the sail down and the rudder off and pulled the centre-board up. There was a big swell breaking on the sandy beach and the boat came in on a wave and I jumped out to stop the boat being sucked out again by the back-wash.

The boat was parallel to the beach and I was between the boat and the beach, keeping the boat very hard with both hands on the side tanks. But the next wave was much bigger than the one before and when it came I realized too late the danger and I only had time to get one leg up off the sand before the wave hit the boat and my left leg broke like a match. It broke both bones so that my foot was absolutely loose and I was floating on the wave onto the sand. I got such a shock and I remember I was thinking that now I would never sail dinghies any more but I was sure I could still sail the *Star-boat* and other keelboats. I thought I would never be ski-ing again and all this flashed through my mind just at that moment.

I pulled myself out of the water and a *Finn* sailor who was a dentist put a piece of wood on to my leg and then he went to get an ambulance near to the place. The natives were drinking coffee and so

In spite of breaking his leg badly in 1966, he nevertheless won two World Championships and just failed to win a third.

Mogens Berger

as he had no time to wait for them to finish he was stealing the ambulance and they were running after him. So he came to the beach driving the ambulance and when I was already on the stretcher the local ambulance people came and then they drove it to the hospital. The dentist helped to get the best doctor to fix my leg. I remember I was

135

crying—I really got a shock—then when I got an injection to be calm—
Oh, then everything was fine and the leg would be good and I could sail
dinghies again. But it was something which hurt a lot and I hope it will
never happen again. Slowly my leg became better and I was able to
sail a keelboat and then a *Finn*. So later I went to Norway for the *5·5-
metre* Gold Cup and the local national races to tune the boat and I
wasn't fast at all, I was just a little slower than the fastest that year and
so I compared their sails and my sails and tried to get the feel of the
boat to see what we should do.

Strit Johansen, my best friend from Cannes, and Paul Mik-Meyer
were crewing and Strit said, "First of all we have to work on the jib and
cut it so that it comes close to the deck and then try to make it with the
same curve from the deck right up to the head". The *5·5-metre* jib is
very tall and narrow and is difficult to set well.

And then I said that our mainsail was too full in the middle and
also we have to bend the mast too much to get that mainsail to set so
let us make all new sails. So we made new sails and I made the jib
rather flat because when I sheeted the jib very close to the deck I could
move the sheet fore and aft and get a nice curve absolutely from the
deck so that the sail was never tight on the foot. There were One Ton
Cup races in Copenhagen at that time and so we went out to try
against the best boats and everything seemed fine. We also tried against
the *Dragons* here and we were much, much faster against them than
we used to be with the old sails. Remember, we were absoutely alone
here, with nobody to tune against. Finally the other *5·5-metres*
arrived and we tried against Robin Aisher and found we were only a little
faster but later we realized he was one of the fastest.

So we started with a four-race series before the World
Championship. We won but people thought we were lucky. In one race
most people went the wrong way but we felt we were fast and so we
won the Cup for the races just before the World Championship and
everybody thought it was pure luck that we won.

Then we started the World Championship and we won the first
race and I remember that as we came into the harbour a *Knaarboat*
sailed in front of us and the skipper asked us "What number?" We put
one finger up and they were laughing—"Gosh! He has been lucky
again." The next day when we came in and they called to us, "What
number?" We put one finger up and repeated this, I think, twice more.
Two races we didn't win. There were six races so we had four firsts, one
second and one sixth.

But we tried very hard to win that World Championship so that before every start we were there one hour early. In the four races that we won we had the wind from the coast, so before the start I was sailing on starboard to see which wind shift gave me the highest direction and which wind shift gave me the lowest. Then I went on to port and watched the coast to note the direction of landmarks to show when I had to tack. So before every start I knew exactly when I should tack and I placed the boat at the start so that I could tack when I wanted. In the first three races before the World Championship I made awful mistakes because I had had no practice in playing with a 5·5-

The 5·5-metre with which he won the World Championship at Copenhagen. Note the jib cut so that the clew is right on the deck.

metre but in the World Championship I really wanted to be the best and because of that I concentrated much, much harder and did beautiful starts in all the races.

Because we knew exactly where to go we never made tactical mistakes. We could sometimes be more or less lucky with the wind because if the wind went back to the mean direction that was bad luck because you couldn't do anything. But the big advantage came when the wind went out to one of the sides because then you can tack and be sure of gaining. But, generally speaking, because we went the right way, and because we had a little better speed than anyone else, then we could do what we liked.

I must say that the best thing for us was that we were three good friends in that boat and, at the same time, we did so well that it was even more fun. One morning, when we started out to the boat, we saw a newspaper with a picture of us all really hanging out. So in the following races, if I really wanted them to hang out I would say "Come on out like in the picture."

In the last race it was blowing very hard but we had already won the World Championship and so it was not necessary for us to start, but because the day before we had come second we really wanted to win this last race. It was blowing very hard and were leading at that time. Strit was bailing the boat and the pump broke. We got so much water in that he said, "Now you will have to slow down because I can't follow you." So I had to point higher and slow down to get the water out of the boat and I was thinking that it was like the old *Finn* days where you had to go right aft in the boat not to get too much water in. It was before we had bailers in the boat and we often had to stop at the windward mark to bail out?

We had a very small dacron spinnaker and we put it up later and seemed to be really planing. We had a speed then that I felt was faster than I had ever had with any dinghy because there were very long waves and very strong wind. I know that this *5·5-metre* had a tremendous speed then because we were sitting high over the water and when you are so high and can still feel the speed, then it must be going fast. In a dinghy when you are planing you are down in the water and you get water in the face and it gives the impression of more speed than there really is. It was amazing to feel how fast the *5·5-metre* could go in some conditions. We won that race and the German came second but because our leach started to stretch longer and longer I couldn't pull in the mainsail. It was block to block so that I couldn't point as high as the German but I put myself in such a position

138

that he could never pass me and we won with quite a bit in hand.

I heard later that some *Star-boat* skippers immediately said, "There you see what sort of class the *5·5-metre* is when a dinghy sailor just can go out and clean them all up. You wait till he gets to the *Star* class." But after the *Star* World Championship in Kiel, I remember the American *5·5-metre* sailor, George O'Day was there with his 3-man keel-boat for the I.Y.R.U. trials and he said to me, "Oh! it was good that you won that too, so now we shall not hear anything more about when you cleaned us out in Copenhagen."

Star World
Championships
at Kiel, 1966

I had the right conditions in Kiel with the *Star* as well. It was blowing hard. In the first three races, we were not fast upwind. We had good starts and we made good tactics but what helped us was that downwind we were planing so much faster than anyone else. John Albrechtson was crewing and had tuned the boat but I said to John, "I'm not going to race that boat any more with that tuning." So for the fourth race we went out of the harbour and I told him to put the mast forward one inch. He put it there but it didn't help and so I told him to put it forward more and he said, "You will break the spreaders." But when we came to the fourth race the boat went like a dream and we were so much faster than anyone else in that particular wind and won easily. We were even able to bear away and pass through the lee of boats ahead and then come up ahead of them.

Then we came to the last race and there I made a big tactical mistake. To win I had to be no more than a maximum of ten places behind Lowell North and a few more places behind the Olympic Silver Medallist Dick Stearns. So my first thought was to put myself near them so that they could never get away more than ten boat lengths from me but I was a little too careful and I got a bad start near North with such a bad wind from an Italian that I couldn't tack and get clear. The tactical mistake was that I was definitely sure that I should have started at the starboard end but North and Dick Stearns started farther down the line and so I felt I had to go down to them.

Because of this bad start I was very far behind and North got nicely away and the people who were starting where I wanted to start were leading. So the right tactic must be that in a *Star* you must start where you really think there is the advantage and then when you are clear then you can go and cover the competitors you have to be near.

Then I really had to work because North was about fifty places ahead of us and so I said to John, "O.K. John, I don't watch him any more. Now we play our own game." I remember on the second beat we went port and were waiting for a good wind shift. We went on and on and on to the port side and it never came and the people who went inshore had very good wind. The fundamental tactic here is that you have to stay—you have to wait.

Then suddenly it came—only a little but it came—a little shift, a little stronger wind, and then I managed to point up and started to gain. But that was the right tactic, really to wait and wait and wait because there was nothing else, no tide or anything. It was the right course because the wind was about the mean and I knew that the wind was going to come back sometime. It was a matter of waiting for it but I was sailing such a long time before the shift came. Then when we came close to the shore the wind started changing very much and that helped me too because I could play on the wind shifts and gained four more boats on the last half beat. So I managed to just make it by one or two places. But that was fun because that made the whole race exciting for the people watching.

If someone wins too easily it's not really fun, not for the winner and not for the others. But, of course, I enjoyed winning almost every race like I did in the *5·5-metres* because there was a special reason for it and I wanted to show that this old boat was not really so slow. But you know in the *Finn,* if it blew more than five metres per second (10 knots) I only had to start and sail round the course. I mean it was only hard work for me—it was not fun.

The *Star* championships were quite different. It was exciting! Oh! lovely, lovely, planing with the *Star* with that huge sail. In competition with other *Stars* it is wonderful but you need a special technique and the main thing is you must trust your rudder because you

must not be afraid to break the rudder. If you are scared of breaking the rudder in the *Star* in strong winds you can't get planing. The main secret of my fast planing in Kiel and other places was that I think I'm harder with my rudder, though the sail also has to be nice and full. But I think most people are afraid to break the rudder. The pressure on the rudder is very hard and most people, I found, are afraid to be so hard on the tiller. They think they will break the boat but it is the only way to keep it going but when you pass a critical point and get more and more speed then the pressure on the tiller becomes less and less but if it starts to luff up you must never let it go up like you can in a dinghy. It is absolutely different from a dinghy. The important thing is that you must keep the pressure on the front of the mainsail. If the *Star* luffs up and the wind disappears from the front part of the mainsail then you are finished, because the pressure on the after half of the sail pushes you

Scandale *rounds the windward mark in the lead in one of the World Championship races at Kiel.*

up into the wind and you can never bear away again.

Of course, you must not be afraid of the boom breaking either and you must have the kicking strap very tight for the very maximum speed on planing. We used to set up the kicking strap very hard but we had a hand on the tackle so that if the boom touched a wave and there was a reasonable chance that the boom would break we could free the kicking strap immediately. When you are planing with a *Star* you make a big wave and there is a hollow just where the boom comes and so if you can keep planing on a *Star* you are making this

Hard wind sailing
in *Stars* and
5·5s

hollow for the boom all the time and you won't break the boom. But if you are afraid and slow down then the boom can touch and break. It is a little like sailing a *Finn* where you also have the long boom and sometimes the tiller is very hard. But it's much easier with the *Star* than the *Finn*, not in technique but because in the *Finn* when you are planing you often can't see anything and you are one hundred per cent sailing by feel because you get so much water in your face that you are blinded. This training in the *Finn* I think has been a great help in being able to plane so fast in the *Star*.

With the *5·5-metre* we were sailing very fast in the last race in the World Championship. You can't really call it planing — it was a kind of surfing — and the technique was to steer precisely and to adjust the sail exactly, because if you go just a little too close you are finished. Remember the rudder on the *5·5-metre* was very near the middle! Once I failed and went too close and the spinnaker collapsed, so you must grip the tiller very hard and steer very precisely. You've got to keep a firm grip on the tiller and force the boat to go where you want it. The *Soling* is easy to steer compared with the *5·5-metre* because of the separate rudder.

It is here that I feel I must include a short article which was written by John Albrechtson and first published in the American magazine *One-Design and Offshore Yachtsman*.

John is Paul's Swedish agent but it was in 1965 that he surprised the *Star* world by invading North America and won the coveted and highly competitive North American Championship.

He later failed to gain selection to represent his Fleet at Kiel and so he sold his boat to Paul and then crewed for him.

Here he sets down his experiences and in a unique way he has captured something of the magic of the "Maestro's" technique.

I first met Paul Elvström at a boat show in Gothenburg in 1963 and was immediately charmed by the legendary and fascinating sailor. Little did I know then that our collaboration over the next couple of years would lead to our victory in the *Star* world championships at Kiel in 1966.

It was on a cold April day that year when I first sat in a sailboat with Paul. He had just launched *Web*, a *5·5-metre* he had borrowed, and

With John Albrechtson in the living room of his house at Hellerup with all the trophies they won together in the Star World Championship *at Kiel. Paul normally does not like trophies, but they won so many this time that they thought it would be fun to have this picture taken.*

we went out for a short tuning spin. I was supposed to sail with him in *Web* during the *5·5* world championships but lack of time forced me to leave my place in the crew to a young Dane. Of course they went on to win the *5·5* title in a very convincing manner.

It was not until I had failed to qualify for the *Star* 'Worlds' representing the Vinga fleet that it was decided that Paul would buy my boat *Scandale*. I was to remain in the boat as crew. It was the same boat with which I had won the North American *Star* championship the year before. The preparation for the 'Worlds' began when I went to Copenhagen with *Scandale* and the Silver Star I had won at the 'North Americans' had to be changed to a red one, because Paul now owned the boat and he had not won a Star class event. At that time I did not dream that the colour would soon be changed again, but to Gold.

In Kiel I noticed how extraordinarily painstaking Paul was in looking after the boat before and between the races. He was always the first to and the last from *Scandale* and there was always something to be done.

In our first work-out I got a shock—a blow in the solar plexus. We rounded the end of the pier in the 20-knot wind and Paul immediately gybed. There was a scream in the mast and shrouds. At sea he didn't show the boat the least of his tenderness or mothercare, but shoved her around mercilessly as though he were riding in a rodeo on a wild mustang.

I was just as shook up as *Scandale,* but realized he was simply driving himself, me and the boat to maximum performance. I had been told that Paul could be compared to a slave merchant when sailing, and I soon realized that this was his way of really testing his equipment to see what we could take—or rather what he calculated we were able to give.

I must point out that it was great sailing with Paul. Naturally it wasn't easy many times to understand his hints and intentions, especially as it was the first time I had sailed as a crew and not as a skipper. You get a quite different perspective as a crew and many times you are left outside the helmsman's thoughts. But most of this confusion was soon straightened out and after a rough beginning the professor proved himself right.

During the first race of the championships the wind was never below 22 knots and the sea was steep. The atmosphere was naturally somewhat tense. I had my eyes open for the best start. With 15 minutes to go I had noticed that the port end of the long line was favoured. It was my opinion and the opinion of almost all the helmsmen that a start near the flag end would be best. This was where all the elite began to gather.

But a couple of minutes before the smoke spurted from the committee boat Paul suddenly changed his mind. Like a bloodhound he had sensed a shift in the wind, and *Scandale* left for the windward

144

flag in order to take off close to the starting ship.

At first I was confused by this fast interpretation and action but my worry eased when I realized that the "Elvström computer" was right. Shortly, we, along with one other boat, had worked out a lead over the rest of the fleet.

I'll never forget that first race. I got my next shock on the first reach after we had rounded the weather mark in second place, about 40 yards astern of the leader. Paul had managed to break the main-sheet traveller on the first leg, so as soon as I got the vang set up I crawled under the afterdeck to fix the traveller controls — a job and a position that is not in keeping with what a crew should be doing on a reach, especially in so much wind.

You can imagine my surprise when I got up and found that we were leading the race and pulling away fast. This was magic. Paul had simply pulled out one of his hidden aces and showed how to sail downwind. He laughed when I asked if there was anything else I could fix under the deck.

These reaches were fantastic. Again I was given a lesson. Paul's way of dominating the reaches by capitalizing on every turn of the wind, and the reading of the waves, made it possible to surf almost constantly.

Under such conditions many *Star-boat* sailors would hesitate to put up the whisker pole. But not Paul. "Set the crochet needle", he would say. (During our training I had fumbled long trying to get the pole end into the jib clew grommet, an exercise that Paul compared with a lady's effort to crochet.)

Paul is very strong and fast. During the gybe he uses his muscles 100 percent, at the same time moving with the agility of an acrobat. He helped me out by loosening one backstay while I was letting go the kicking strap at just the right moment and then setting up the other backstay.

I have often been asked what we actually talked about during races, and many have suggested that it must be hard for a Dane and a Swede to communicate. Danish isn't too hard for a Swede to under-stand, and as Paul is in Sweden quite often and I go to Copenhagen frequently we have worked out a form of "Scandinavian". In tight situations when you have to shout harsh words to competitors we use English, since it is the accepted language at sea. Concerning the terminology, I think that Captain Bligh of the Bounty would have been delighted if he could have used some of the expressions Paul used on certain occasions.

145

Right after the start of the fourth race I fell overboard. In the last fraction of a second I succeeded in catching the backstay with my foot. When I was well back aboard Paul asked me with a smile: "Now, do you intend to stay aboard for the whole race?"

The Elvström method of tuning a boat is both interesting and remarkable. You really learn a lot. His desire to win and his geniality I have already mentioned, but I was also stunned by his fearlessness in executing rather extensive alterations when he thought that something wasn't in order even though we were on top and, in my opinion, we only needed a fraction of an inch change here or there. Between the third and fourth races the mast was taken down for the fourth time since the series began. Some of the stays were shortened about half an inch and the mast was moved two inches at the bottom. Early next morning we were out tuning and the mast was moved an additional three inches before Paul was satisfied with the balance of the boat.

During this tune-up we had sailed against an average boat and on the way out to the starting line I couldn't help telling Paul that I was very anxious to find out what such a radical change had done to the boat when we got up against the "big guys". Paul admitted the possibility of his fallibility when he said "You can bet that I'm as curious about it as you are."

Directly after the start we got a wonderful lead in the heavy going, with Paul sailing beautifully. We won the race with a good margin and again Paul had taught a lesson and then proved it was right. That night we left *Scandale* as she was.

The last race was something like a nightmare and in the lighter weather we made our worst start of the series and in addition we were faced with trying to watch our three closest competitors. During the first windward leg Paul wanted to head out to sea where one of them had gone right after the start. However we found that Lowell North and Dick Stearns were on the other side of the course. The result was that we tried to beat up the leg in between. We soon discovered that we were a long way from first place. When the last upwind leg began we had to pass at least half a dozen boats in the fading wind.

Paul decided immediately to head away on a long port tack and asked worriedly many, many times how we were doing compared to the starboard bunch. This showed that even "the master of the seas" can get nervous and uncertain. At the end of the leg the wind started to shift back and forth but Paul capitalized on the changes with fantastic precision. Typical of his constant struggle for perfection was that he got angry on the last run when Pelle Petterson of Sweden passed us, although our place was still good enough to win the series. At the end, of course, all was happiness.

That night there were many nice words spoken about Paul and the way we had won the regatta, and Paul said that he had never experienced such exaltation as this time. And never before had we seen such trophies — both in number and size.

I mentioned earlier how Paul was always shocking me. The third shock came on the way to the presentation dinner when *Scandale* got loose from the back of the station wagon when we were travelling at 50 m.p.h. The trailer rolled on by itself for about 50 yards and parked alongside a brick wall. *Scandale* didn't get a scratch. Paul had said after the last race: "It's strange but I always have a great deal of luck at the big championships".

With his crew, Paul Mik-Meyer, after winning his second Star World Championship in 1967.

147

Bruce Kirby is one of the world's top dinghy sailors and is currently the most sought-after designer in the *International Fourteen foot* class. He is a man of the wide experience which his job as Editor of the internationally famous 'One-Design and Offshore Magazine' demands. He used to be a journalist on the 'Montreal Star' but joined 'One-Design' almost at its birth and has helped to build it up to its present unique position amongst yachting magazines.

Bruce represented his native Canada in the 1956 Olympics in the *Finn* class and again at Tokyo in 1964. He is also a fine *Star* sailor and sailed for Canada in this class in Acapulco. He has also sailed and raced all sorts of craft ranging from 12-Metres and ocean racers down to *International Fourteens*.

The following commentary represents the opinions of an incredulous and hard-to-convince journalist who was immediately charmed and then impressed by this quite outstanding character. His views **are** representative of a great many North Americans.

A measure of a man's genius

Kirby. As he ground out his narrow victory in the world *Star* championships in 1966 the tremendous effort Paul Elvström expended ashore outweighed even the brilliance of his helmsmanship; and surely this is the measure of his genius as the world's leading sailor. On the race course he is able to recognize a defect in rig, sails or tuning which is costing him six or eight boatlengths in a 10-mile race. While sailing the boat he determines what must be done to cure the defect; then when he goes ashore he effects the cure.

After almost every race of this hard weather, five-race series, when everyone else was getting in out of the wicked blast as soon as possible, Elvström and his crew, John Albrechtson, were out there trying to find a way to improve their performance, if ever so slightly. The mast was out of their boat almost daily, stay lengths were altered, tensions were changed. After the third race, in which the Dane had finished second, he decided the mast position, bend and rake were entirely wrong for the prevailing air. So he moved the spar forward no less than five inches at the step, somewhat less at the deck, increased the rake, altered the stays to reduce bend, and then went out and won the next race.

On the sailing course Elvström was remarkable off the wind in a *Star.* When he got around the top mark he took command completely. Before the others had their boom vangs properly down Elvström was through their lee and into the lead. He would be a minute ahead by the end of the second reach. But if Elvström was good on the reaches he was more outstanding on the dead runs. This is the point of sailing on which the *Star* is at its worst. It has a long, low boom which makes it difficult to pull the twist out of the sail with the "go fast". So the sail tends to twist at the top and cause heavy rolling to windward. Gybing accidentally is an ever-present danger. If the boom rolls under it is likely to snap off. If the roll is to windward the boat might gybe and broach in the same motion, and if the whisker pole is on when this happens, the clew of the jib will go under and the resulting pressure transmitted along the whisker pole to the mast may well push the mast out of column and cause it to buckle.

It is under such conditions that Elvström shines. While others do what they can to prevent all of the above catastrophes he aims his boat straight downwind and sails, apparently unperturbed, for the finish line. Sailing by the lee in heavy weather with impunity is a *Finn*-sailor's talent which Elvström has carried over to the *Star*. And it appears that, as he improved the breed in *Finns* by leading the way with better techniques, so he already has been able to show the *Star* pundits a trick or two they had not managed to pick up in the 55 years of their history.

In 1966 Paul Elvström won the world championships of the *Star* class and the *5·5* class and finished a close second in the *5-0-5* championships. In years gone by he won the world title in *Snipes, Finns, Flying Dutchman* and *5·5s*. Now he has yet again shown his absolute genius by capturing the first World *Soling* Championship against the most medal-bestrewn and talented fleet ever.

As his world titles have encompassed five Olympic classes plus two top non-Olympic classes, he must surely be called the world's best helmsman. There is absolutely no reason to doubt that this broad-shouldered, bespectacled Dane could win the championship of any class.

As a competitor I have had the privilege of sailing against him in *Finns* (1956 Olympics) and in *Stars* (the World Championships at Kiel) and as a journalist I have had the duty to know what he has been up to during his long career as the best sailor who has ever turned his hand to the sport. There is little doubt that no-one, in any sport, has ever had the success that Elvström has enjoyed. On top of his world titles his four Olympic Gold Medals in single-handed sailing meant that he had stayed on top for 12 years in this class, which is an Olympic record in any game. And I can remember thinking during the 1956 Games, when I had the opportunity to attend many of the track and

149

Part of the 90-strong Soling *fleet at the World Championship which was won by Paul Elvström.*

An editor's opinion

field events with Elvström (after the day's sailing was over) that if he had decided to concentrate on virtually any other sport he would have been on top there too.

It goes without saying that this man knows the sport of sailing better than anyone else. With his success as a sailboat racer and businessman Elvström has frequently been accused of taking the whole thing too seriously. Those who don't know him think of him as a computer which has been programmed to win races.

Nothing could be further from the truth. For along with the fanatical desire and will to win goes a broad intelligence and a sense of humour which never fails to come to the fore regardless of the situation.

When I first knew Elvström, in 1956, his command of the English language was impressive, but limited. The thing which makes the man tick is confidence, without bragging or vanity, and at that time he knew only a very direct form of English. The best example of it came at the end of the Olympics when he had won very decisively and was being interviewed by an Australian journalist who asked the obvious question: "To what do you attribute your victory?" Elvström answered: "The others—they were too slowly."

150

An extrovert
champion with a
sense of humour

Coming from a small country Elvström has had to sail with many persons who do not speak his native tongue. And the stories he has to tell about regattas with "foreign" crews or skippers can keep him going for hours. In a recent *Star* "worlds" his crew was John Albrechtson, a Swede. Elvström's Swedish is quite good; Albrechtson's Danish is not too good; but they both speak English well.

So (as Albrechtson tells it) the race starts off in Swedish. All is calm and all is understood. Then, as things get somewhat more tense, the language changes to English and communications begin to suffer. Then, when the chips are down and Elvström wants something done quicker than now, he switches to Danish and the result is chaos. Now add to this 30—40 mph winds, heavy seas and a *Starboat!* So for those who think the Great Dane's success has been won at the expense of being human, and humorous, rest assured that this is not the case. For if Elvström may be called the "only true sailing genius" he must also be called gentleman, sportsman and "good guy".

Paul is one of the few people I have met who overshadows his reputation. He is almost always better than you expect him to be, even though you already know he is the best in the world.

When he won his first gold medal he was unknown outside Denmark. So when the 1952 Olympics came along he was the defending champ, but who could possibly win two Olympic Gold Medals in a row?

He won that year by a comfortable margin in medium to heavy airs. Then came the 1956 Games at Melbourne where the wind was expected to blow ... and did. That year he had five firsts in the seven races to take his third Olympic Gold Medal. It was, I believe, the first time anyone in any sport had won a gold medal three times in a row.

With the 1960 Games organized for the Bay of Naples, where the winds are usually light to medium and tricky, the Elvström victory string was expected to end. After all he was now in his 30s; he had taught his techniques to the world, and with the Olympics in Italy, which is a very central location, there would obviously be a large entry. There were 35 entries—the biggest ever—and Elvström won so decisively that he didn't have to sail the final race.

Elvström retired from active international and Olympic sailing after the 1960 Games and has only recently come back to plague us with his genius. But during those early years while he was busy winning four straight Olympic Gold Medals, he also found time to win world championships in other classes too.

Paul is the classic example of drive and desire combined with skill. He is the type of person who should win Olympic medals because he tries harder. There are many who think Elvström is good because he's a sailmaker. But it's really the other way around. He's a sailmaker because he's good, and he won his first two Olympic titles while he was still in the building construction business.

I feel entirely confident in saying, without reservation, that he is the greatest small boat helmsman who ever lived. And I feel equally confident that he has done more to improve the calibre of sailing the world over than any other man.

In Australia in 1956 when Elvström won his third straight Gold Medal, I had the opportunity to watch him in action. It was three days before the Olympic sailing events were to begin and most of the boys in the *Finn* group were making final adjustments to hiking straps, mainsheet rigs and leg padding. As usual the wind was blowing about 25 to 30 knots from the south-west. One or two of the *Finn* sailors were out practising.

One of these was Paul Elvström, the Dane. Although we had only been practising in our craft for a few days Elvström had already become a legend. Seldom was he referred to by name. It was usually either "The Great Dane" or "The Red Devil", for he always wore red sweaters and red sweat pants. In the practice skirmishes no one had been able to stay near him in this heavy going, and if the weather remained rugged there seemed no reason to believe he would not take his third straight gold medal in the monotype class.

The strong wind was blowing almost straight into the harbour; the ramps where the *Finns* were lined up were on a lee shore. Someone said, "Here comes the 'red devil' ". We all looked up and Elvström was about 100 yards off, planing on a very broad port tack reach. He was standing up in the boat. As we watched, he did a quick gybe; the boat did not stop planing, and the mast never left the perpendicular. Now he was planing along on the starboard tack on very nearly the same course as before.

In his high-pitched voice, and in the sing-song Danish language, he was shouting something to his good friend and spare man, Bjorg Schwarz who was preparing to take one of the *Finns* out to do battle with his countryman. Three more times Elvström gybed his *Finn* as he planed towards the ramps. The manoeuvres were so smooth he might have been doing them in a five knot breeze. The only apparent move Elvström made was to duck when the boom came over. He was holding all parts of the sheet in one hand and the tiller in the other. The tiller was scarcely used at all. With only a very slight change of course, he would pull the sail across and keep on blasting along. About 15 feet from the ramps Elvström wheeled his boat into the wind, got his instructions across to Schwarz, and then sailed off again into rugged Port Phillip Bay.

This anecdote from the Olympics doesn't prove very much; it is merely a word picture of the world's best small boat sailor in action. The episode meant no more to Elvström than a cup of tea to an Englishman. He probably didn't have to make those four gybes in about 40 seconds and why he did is a matter of conjecture. He practices very hard, and there is a good chance that this was simply part of a practice session; maybe he was just showing off. That's quite possible and it was certainly a worth-while show. There is a strong possibility too that he was trying to discourage his competition before the racing began, and if that is the case then he did an excellent job. I for one had never before watched a more skilful sailing manoeuvre and admitted to myself that I could not go out directly and copy it. Gybing in a *Finn* dinghy four times in 40 seconds in a 25-knot wind is quite a feat in itself, but to do it without even mussing your hair, and without missing a syllable of a shouted conversation is nothing short of fantastic.

That was one of my first good looks at Elvström in action. During the following two weeks we saw him walk off with five of the seven races in the Olympic competition to receive his third first place award in eight years.

We had all heard of this Dane before going to Australia. For years— ever since he had won his first gold medal in England in the 1948 Games —I had heard stories about his ability and his devotion to the sport. The stories that filtered through to North America about this fellow were many, and most of them quite startling. Like any stories which have come a long way and been told many times, I was inclined to take these Elvström anecdotes with many grains of salt. There was never any doubt in my mind that the man was good; but I refused to believe that he was a superman. Frequently one has the opportunity in life to prick the bubble of reputation which has grown round a famous man. Almost invariably it is possible to find weaknesses in the legendary expert, no matter what his field.

But I must admit with full conviction that the "Great Dane" lived up to anything and everything I had ever heard about him. He did not let down his reputation. The most fantastic tales about his skill, devotion and stamina were verified time and again during those weeks in Australia.

153

Eight

Sailmaking and boat tuning

The universal sail

I think that advances can still be made with the *Finn* sail, which has had a tremendous lot of development over the years. What we are looking for is to find one mast and one sail which goes at maximum speed under all conditions and that's so difficult that what we have found today has not yet reached that ideal. I am sure we will find it one day with another mast and another cloth and another sail design. The cloth is very, very important in a sail. The sail shape is a combination of the cloth and the shape you cut into that sail. If you use a different cloth you've got to cut the sail slightly differently to compensate for the qualities of the cloth.

The cloth we can get today is very variable in elasticity and density and it produces different shapes. For instance in the *Finn,* if you use too stiff a cloth and the mast is bending, the sail shape forward normally becomes too flat very quickly. If you use too soft a cloth generally speaking it will become too baggy in more wind. What we find today is that we use a medium cloth and when you bend your mast you stretch your luff with the cunningham hole. In this way the natural bag the wind pressure gives the sail is moved forward nearer the mast. But the mast is bending more and this takes it out again. So you keep the same position of maximum flow in light winds and strong winds. Also making the leach elastic helps by not making the sail too baggy in strong winds. We have found today that the thinner the yarn is on the weft, that is across the cloth, the less diagonal elasticity the cloth has. If you use a cloth with the same yarn in both directions you have an inelastic leach but you have more diagonal elasticity which is bad for a *Finn* sail.

There are two ways that you can adjust the stretchiness of the leach and one is to sew the panels together so that the wefts are at a

Cloth types

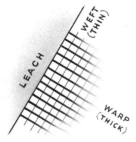

154

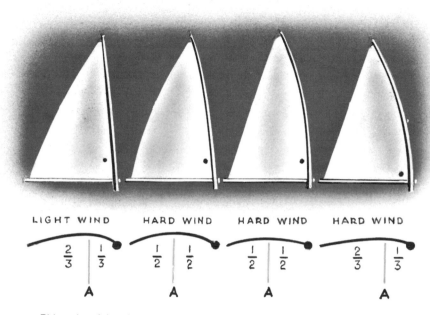

LIGHT WIND	HARD WIND	HARD WIND	HARD WIND
$\frac{2}{3}$ $\frac{1}{3}$	$\frac{1}{2}$ $\frac{1}{2}$	$\frac{1}{2}$ $\frac{1}{2}$	$\frac{2}{3}$ $\frac{1}{3}$
A	A	A	A

This series of drawings shows the progressive use of mast bend and Cunningham hole in moving from a light wind to a hard wind. On the left in the light wind the position of the maximum flow, A, is normal. In the second diagram there is a hard wind and the flow has moved aft. In the third diagram still in a hard wind the mast has been bent reducing the amount of flow but the position is the same. In the fourth diagram the mast is bent and the Cunningham hole is pulled down which pulls the position of maximum flow forward.

The elastic leach

very slight angle to the line of strain between the end of the boom and the head of the mast, and the other is by choosing a cloth which stretches a bit on the weft. We try to use both methods since they both help the elasticity of the leach especially in the hard puffs because there you cannot adjust the luff quickly enough but the elasticity in the leach does open it automatically. Instead of easing the sheet the stretchy leach frees automatically but it is difficult to make it elastic enough.

With a cloth the ideal is to make the weft direction elastic enough and the diagonal elasticity as little as possible. I want a cloth that is not too stiff and a diagonal elasticity that is small, but this is very difficult to get.

Today we have only the woven cloth but I am sure one day we will find a new material, a kind of plastic which doesn't become stiff in

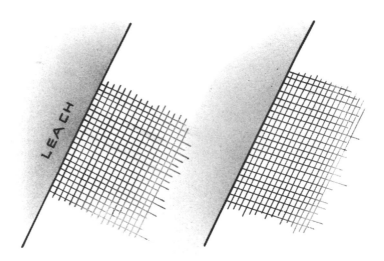

With the cloths sewn at a slight bias angle it distorts diagonally slightly when under tension and thus stretches.

New materials

cold weather and we may not sew sails any more but we will make them on big moulds. So to produce a sail we will make a mould of the right shape. When this new material comes maybe it will be such that we can't bend the mast because it will be too stiff or perhaps it will only be an advantage to bend the mast very little. Perhaps we will put up the sail and then adjust the mast exactly.

Flexibility

I don't know whether this business of the mast bending, or perhaps better, flexing, is a good thing apart from the way you can adjust the sail shape. There are two different things here, bending and flexing. Bending in order to alter the sail and flexing to allow for taking up shock when you hit a wave or when a puff hits you. We can't say exactly what is the fastest because it's different in every boat and is different downwind and upwind and we must always compromise.

Sailmaking is a compromise

For instance, let us say we produce a *Finn* sail shape which is much faster downwind and a little slower than the fastest shape upwind. Then maybe on a racing course this boat generally wins so much downwind and loses very little upwind in certain conditions, that this sail will be the fastest when racing on this course. It is the same with the flexibility of the rig or the hull. You have to find the fastest combination. I don't think anyone can tell what is best. We can only try small variations and find what is the fastest. Maybe a soft hull is very fast when planing on a certain boat because it alters the shape to a better planing hull but perhaps it is a little slower upwind. Nevertheless we may find that we can have an overall advantage by building it in that way. So from my experience there is no rigid rule which says that a mast or a rig or a boat should be flexible or stiff.

The *C class* catamaran rig with a wing mast is definitely the fastest because it keeps the most effective shape all the way up and the sail does not twist and that is a big advantage. They found in one American challenge that they had to introduce a little twist in the sail of the American boat because they found that they couldn't trim the sail accurately enough. But this was a weakness of the skipper and not

The "C" class Catamaran Opus *which Paul took to England but could find no one except the Australian challenger to race against. He felt afterwards that this boat was about the same speed as the British defender.*

the rig. This takes us back to the business of sailing *Dragons* or keelboats where you have to have more twist in the sail because the boat is moving about and you can't steer it precisely. If we could have a super-man who could steer the boat accurately or maybe a computer to do it then I think the aerofoil shape all the way up would be bound to win.

When I sailed the *C class* catamaran we were fast when we tested against other boats but we could have been much faster because I had no practice at steering so accurately. Maybe on this cat a wind indicator would be a great help so that it would become partly automatic to steer. In this cat it is more important to keep the wind at the right angle to the mast than the boat to be easy in the sea.

This is the fascinating thing about sailing. There are so many variables and everything is different in every boat and on each course that nobody can be really precise and probably never will be.

In the old days with the *Finn* we were only thinking about the sail shape and how the mast affected it. We didn't know that we would go so fast when the mast was soft near the boom. We knew way back in about '57 or '58 that to go to windward we had to have the boom right

on the deck, even in light winds. Therefore we raked the mast in light winds so that when we had the boom on the deck the mast didn't bend so much and then we raked it more upright in strong winds so that with the boom still on the deck it bent more, but when we raked the mast too much backwards it was a disadvantage on the run. So what the younger generation recently found was that if they made the mast soft just by the boom they are able to sail with an upright mast downwind, and then when they sheet in hard the boom comes to the deck and so

158

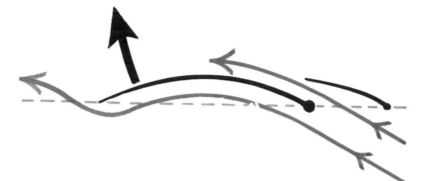

*Full mainsail, flat jib.
The stern is pushed to
leeward.*

they are also fast upwind. I think no one can tell why it's faster when you've got the boom on the deck but it is so and we have to accept it.

In a *Dragon*, where you have a back-stay you still want the sail to do the bending and not the back-stay. If the mast adjusts the sail then the mast bends automatically when the sail receives a hard puff. If you want an open leach in a hard puff you can rig the mast to do it. But take the *Star-boat*, there you don't want an open leach in a hard puff because if the leach freed it would give lee helm. In a very strong wind an open leach on a *Star* will give lee helm and the boat will not go fast or tack. This lee helm can also be because the jib is too full. A flat jib in a strong wind will help and the jib on the *Star* has to be flat compared with jibs on other boats.

So again with the flexibility of the mast, bending the mast by the back-stay, or by the sail itself it is compromise and you can't say anything general. In the *Soling* class for instance, you have to have a tight

**Mast bending
on a keelboat**

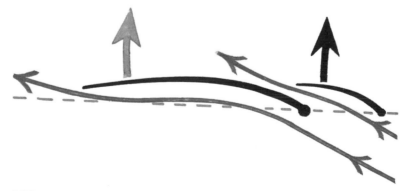

*Flat mainsail, full jib.
The bow is pushed to
leeward.*

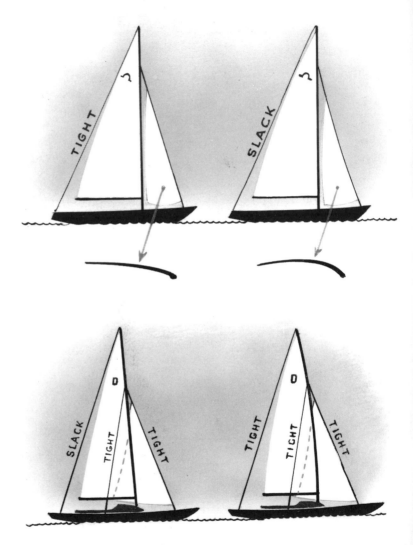

Altering the shape of the Soling *jib.*

Altering the shape of the Dragon *mainsail.*

Adjusting the back-stay

back-stay to keep the fore-stay tight. But if the jib is very flat you have to loosen the back-stay to give more shape to the jib. You even have to do this when you are going to windward in a light wind.

It's the same with the *Star* where you can have a flat jib and if you don't pull in the runners tight you can have a better curve. The more the wind comes the more you pull in the runners, in that way you can keep the same jib shape in light winds and strong winds. In the *Soling* you can adjust the fore-stay by the back-stay and if the jib is too baggy you must always keep the back-stay tight.

A tight fore-stay normally is a big advantage in strong winds on *5·5-metres* and *Solings* It is very important you arrange the back-stay so that you really can pull as hard as you like. If you find it a big advantage to have that particular fore-stay tight then you have to have the back-stay very tight too. Then of course you are bending your mast and if you can't stiffen up the mast to match the mainsail you have then you must change the mainsail to one which has a bigger mast curve.

Tension on the fore-stay

In a *Dragon* you use the runners to tighten the fore-stay. The back-stay is only used when you are gybing. The runners don't help much in light and medium winds but when the wind comes stronger and stronger the more important the runners become.

You can adjust the mainsail leach a little with the backstay and also you can tighten up the jumpers hard and then tighten the back-stay and so make the *Dragon* mast stiff sideways in that way. You may find with the sail that you are using that you want it very stiff sideways, but generally speaking I prefer the top of the *Dragon* mast to be a little elastic without tension on the back-stay. So in a hard puff the top of the mast will bend sideways and back automatically and not only open the leach but make the distance from the top of the mast to the end of the boom smaller, which will work nearly the same as if you eased the mainsheet a little in a hard puff.

Looking at the headsail

I think most helmsmen don't look at their genoa or jib enough because it is partly hidden, especially the most important bit of it, behind the mainsail. Skippers should get off their boat and have a look at their own boat sailing from outside. I think that from a power boat watching a race in their own class helmsmen can see the differences from boat to boat and can watch how the winner sheets the sails on his boat. He can go to the fastest boat and watch his sheeting, his sail shape, how he adjusts everything. Instead of racing against him for fifty races and seeing nothing, in only one race he can learn a lot and he can try to copy. It would save him a lot of time.

161

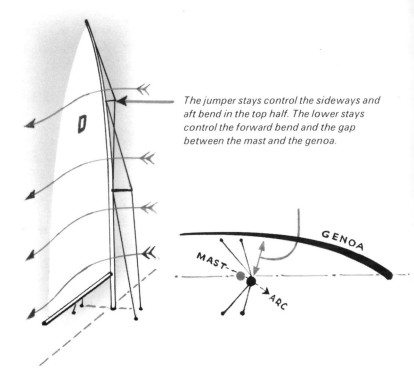

The jumper stays control the sideways and aft bend in the top half. The lower stays control the forward bend and the gap between the mast and the genoa.

Looking at your headsail

If there is something wrong with your boat you really want to get someone else to sail it in a race so that you can compare. People take too little notice of their jib or genoa because they can't see it so well. They think the mainsail is everything. It's a natural failing. But remember the smaller the jib is the more important the mainsail becomes, and the bigger the foresail becomes the less important is the mainsail. In ocean racing you can sometimes take the mainsail down and you won't feel anything is missing. It's a good idea sometimes to take the mainsail off and leave the genoa or jib up and have a good look at it from where you are sailing the boat. You won't tell anything regarding the speed but you can see the shape of the sail.

Take a *Dragon* which has a big genoa—you will have a good view without the mainsail and if you have problems you'll see what to do. You can take the sailmaker and say, "I would like to try it flatter here or fuller there or fuller all over, or another leach. Is it possible?" and then if he says "Yes, we can do that". Then you can try it.

You cannot say by just looking at a genoa if it is fast or not

162

Leaches and leach lines

because my experience is that when people try to tell me that this sail is too full or too flat or it is so-and-so, they have nothing to compare it with. It gives me a wrong picture of what they are talking about and so when people talk about a sail I always say, "I must see the sail myself before I can take any decision on it". Everybody knows the obvious faults like a flapping leach or a hooking leach and most people can normally tell whether the fairlead is in roughly the right position — causing too much backwind on the mainsail by being too far forward or not drawing properly at the head of the jib because it is too far aft.

I would say that the sail may have a leach line to stop flapping, but when you tighten the line the leach will curl and then the big question is whether it is better to leave the leach flapping, or is it better to stop it, even if it does curl. But when we do this, it seems to make no difference, so it must be that both flapping and curling are bad because they can't both be good.

But what we have found is that we can make the leach very light so that, when it flaps, it is not really flapping but only has a light vibration. The heavier the leach is made by folding cloth, then the more heavily it flaps. So I think that a heat-cut leach, rather than a tabled leach, is probably a better way of making it, but the life of it is not very long.

But if you really want the best compromise in a particular series of races, I think a light tabling made by folding the cloth only 5 mm will make a light leach that is also strong.

A heat-cut leach is not strong, but I think it is the fastest, but when it overstretches it's quite simple to take tucks in it, to take it up again to the original shape.

On the left is a typical curling leach. In the centre is an overstretched leach which is flapping. On the right you can see what happens when you tighten the leach line.

On the left a tabled leach can flap very heavily. In the centre a leach turned only five millimetres can flap lightly. On the right a heat cut leach will only flap very lightly indeed.

163

People often don't realize how a sail changes shape a little at a time during its whole life. It happens so slowly that they sometimes wonder why the performance is falling off. If they think it has changed shape, then they are right, because a lot of cloth shrinks and this means that the whole sail becomes flatter. So the sail which was very good in a certain condition, has become slow. Sunlight can shrink some types of cloth. I don't know exactly why, but it must be something in the finishing of the cloth which makes it shrink. For instance, you can finish a cloth by shrinking, so that when you heat it up it shrinks, and if you don't do it enough then I think that the sun can complete or continue the process, and then the sail becomes too flat. But, if the sail is cut too baggy and it becomes flatter, then this will only help, and maybe it becomes faster under certain conditions.

So the skipper has got to be really very perceptive, he's got to try to decide whether his sail is at its peak when new or is going to reach its peak after a month or two's sailing, and he's got to try to notice with an open mind whether the sail is losing its power or whether it's just he, the skipper, who is losing his concentration. The experienced skipper should know if the sail shape is good, and if everything else is perfect. Most people are steering a boat nearly in the same way, so the sail shape and tuning are so very important.

In any class if you go out with the wrong sail you have no chance at all. In the *Star* class, because the sail is so big compared to the size of the boat and compared to the weight of the crew, the sail is the main factor. On the *Star* if the mainsail is made with the leach closed it is not necessary to sheet in hard to keep a nice shape and when you don't sheet hard it seems that everything is more elastic and the draft in the sail is more effective.

I think that a lot of people confuse the English that we use when describing a sail, for instance supposing we take the words "a tight leach". Many people mean by "a tight leach" a leach which I normally call a "closed" leach. In other words the flow is far aft in the sail and therefore the leach part of the sail comes up to windward a bit. That's what I call a sail which is "closing". It is like an aeroplane when it's going down for landing with its flap down.

When we talk about "sheeting the sail in hard" this makes what we can also call a "tight" leach, but here we are thinking more of the tension in the leach because when you pull the mainsail down hard the cloth between the end of the boom and the top of the mast becomes tighter. Normally it is a bad thing to have this cloth very tight.

Therefore I make a *Dragon* sail with the flow aft so that the leach

164

A "tight" leach and a "closed" leach

closes a little near the bottom especially. To keep a nice shape I needn't sheet the sail in hard and therefore I needn't get the cloth tight along the leach. So, if I sheet it in hard you will find the sail too tight on the leach and the boat stops, but if I ease the sheet the sail will get the perfect shape we all know—a fair curve. But if the leach is not closed enough then you have to sheet hard to get it "closed" and then this also "tightens" it which can be bad. I mean that if I sheet the sail in harder the cloth along the leach becomes tighter which has the effect of "closing" the leach slightly. But that is a bad combination because though I've got the shape, in other words the leach is "closing" enough to make the sails fuller, the tension of the leach is bad because it is not elastic enough.

Sheeting the *Dragon* mainsail

We all know that if we tighten the mainsheet too hard, the boat is too difficult to steer, because the sail all the way up has the same angle to the wind, so you have to steer more precisely than is possible in waves. It's all right in smooth water because you can balance the boat accurately, but if there are any waves you can't keep the sail working at the correct angle. At the same time if you sheet in too hard you probably also make the sail too flat and then the boat won't go through the waves, so it stops.

We are thinking here mainly of keelboats, but it can be the same with a dinghy sometimes. A dinghy, especially a trapeze dinghy is

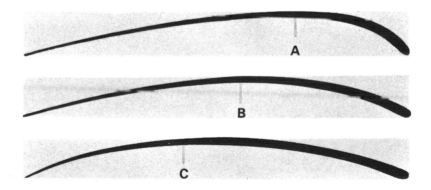

These three sails have the same maximum depth of flow. Sail A has a "free" or "open" leach. It is only useful in hard winds and you cannot point very high. Sail B is a normal medium and light wind sail and you can point quite high. Sail C has a "tight" or "closed" leach. You can point very high especially in light winds with this sail but in stronger winds it has too much drag and can produce weather helm.

165

something between a catamaran and a keelboat. The trapeze dinghy is a faster boat and therefore you can sheet it harder. The catamaran you can sheet very hard indeed. Thinking again of a keelboat, you can't sheet a heavy, wide boat so hard as a *12-metre* or a *Soling* or a *5·5-metre*. So it means that you have to make a different sort of sail for different sorts of boats.

In my opinion, you can never tell what shape is the most effective on any particular boat. You can say that a sail has to be a certain shape and we can prove that this is the most effective shape from wind tunnels and theory, but remember in practice the shape of the sail on every boat is a compromise between the design of the boat and the rig, because the two sails have to work together and the two sails have to work on that boat with that keel and tiller. So you can probably never use the most effective shape on both the genoa and the mainsail.

If the most effective shape, for instance, makes the boat carry weather helm and you cannot move the mast, the boat will never go. You must compromise to make a sail shape which will give a light tiller.

Let us think of an ocean racer with a big genoa. Nothing will disturb that genoa from the lee side and so you can make it the most effective shape on its own. But the mainsail is a compromise because you can't make it an ideally effective shape. You have to make it so that it doesn't become too disturbed by the genoa or so that it doesn't introduce weather helm. You could say that in an ocean racer we can never make the mainsail of the most effective shape that we can find from wind tunnels and our experience. I made a *Dragon* genoa for a Swedish owner in a rather soft cloth and in a medium wind no one could beat this boat. No genoa was faster than that one and even when it was six years old it was still his fastest genoa. When I realized that it was really true that whatever he put up this old genoa was still the fastest in medium winds, I looked at it and found that in winds from 4–7 metres per second (8–14 knots), the cloth was stretching to a certain shape which was tremendously effective. This then helped me to discover that a *Dragon* genoa should have a very fair curve and the maximum bag should be just near the middle.

If the mast on the boat is too far aft and the rules permit it to be there and no where else, then you must make a fuller genoa. At the same time you can't make the mainsail the most effective shape but instead you have to open the leach so that it doesn't press the stern to leeward and increase the load on the tiller. So the sail shape is a compromise and every single class has to have a different sail design to be able to make that particular boat fast. Only for a boat with one

The boat carries too much weather helm.
The mainsail is too full and presses the stern
to leeward.

The mainsail is made flatter and the foresail
is made fuller and the boat is now balanced

With this boat the class rules say that the
mast must be in this position which is too far
forward. The boat carries lee helm. The
remedy is to make the mainsail fuller and the
jib flatter, and the boat is then balanced.

In a Star boat the mainsail is so big it is the
most important factor in balance.

In an ocean racer the genoa is so big that it is
the most important sail.

167

mast which turns and only one sail can you make the most effective
shaped sail.

A simple example of this compromise could be that you can make
a *Finn* sail, for example, which is very full in the lower part, but you
couldn't use that sort of sail today on a *Flying Dutchman* because of the
back-wind·of the genoa when you are going to windward. But you can
make the *Flying Dutchman* genoa like a *Finn* mainsail because it is
working in undisturbed air.

Another thing about sails, not only do you have to make special
sails for each type of boat, depending on the boat's characteristics and
the rules that govern the class, but you have to make sails for different
conditions of wind and sea. One sail design is fast in a certain wind
strength and certain conditions and slow in another type of conditions.
We all know that but the same sail can also be slower in one place than
another but in the same wind strength and then it must only be because
of the difference in the sea conditions. It seems that maybe you have
to be careful if you're an international sailor, to choose the right sail for
the water you are using.

On the left in light winds and smooth sea you can use flat sails and point high.
On the right in a rough sea you have to use full sails and you cannot point so high.

In the '68 Olympics I was expecting lighter winds and we had a
rig tuned for light winds. This meant that my sail was fuller forward and
the leach was more open so that I could sheet it closer. But in the wind
and waves which we had, if I sheeted in so that I could point then I had
not enough speed. And if I eased the mainsail then I could not point.
My leach should have been more closed so that I could ease the sail
for the speed and yet I could still point.

Now let us consider a little about the hull and rig tuning. I have a
good story which demonstrates the need for stiffness in a hull. When I
took part in the *Snipe* class World Championship in Santander, in
Spain, in '54 I think, I borrowed a new fibre-glass *Snipe* which was very
soft in the bottom and whatever we did with it it was hopeless.
Especially on planing it was so slow that I have never seen anything
like it, but I knew a sister boat to the one I borrowed. The owner

stiffened up the hull and then the boat changed from a slow boat to a very fast boat. So my experience with a *Snipe* is that the hull has to be very stiff. Let us say it has to be stiff enough because if it is stiffer than that then the extra stiffness doesn't have any effect of course.

I had the same experience with the *5-0-5,* the *Flying Dutchman* and the *Finn*. My experience with a *Finn* has always been that it had to be as stiff as possible to be able to plane fast, except that I once had a French Lanaverre *Finn* and I know it was very flat on the keel-line, and that helps a lot on planing, but at the same time it was very soft but nothing could keep up with this boat on planing whoever was sailing it.

I mentioned before the *Flying Dutchman* in which we won the World Championship. It was a soft boat but I must say we were awfully slow and so I have the feeling that the *Flying Dutchman* has to be stiff also.

I had a *5-0-5* for the World Championship in '57 which was 30 kilos too heavy, and it was tremendously fast upwind, but because of the weight it started planing later than anybody else but the hull was very stiff. Later when I got a fibre-glass *5-0-5* which was much softer I was planing all right but this boat was on absolute minimum weight and it was not fast in strong winds upwind. If this light boat had been stiffer but still with minimum weight, I am sure it would have been so much faster. What this proves is that the hull has to be stiff and that was the reason why some boats are good even if they are too heavy.

It is my experience, and most international dinghy sailors say the same, that the centreboard must be very stiff—as stiff as it can be made. Of course, you must also take care that it is not going to be too heavy. It must not be sloppy in the centreboard case and you can test this if you heel the boat over on the ground and pull the centreboard out. You can try to press the centreboard up and down, and I think that the best centreboard case is one which does not allow any side movement at all.

In the *5-0-5* I put wood on the aft edge of the centreboard at the top so that the forward edge could move from side to side—the part where the centreboard pivot bolt went through the board. The front edge could move from side to side when we tacked, but the aft edge could not move at all. I have the same experience in the *Flying Dutchman* and in nearly all other boats that every centreboard must be very stiff.

Now in the case of the *5-0-5,* which is a class where you are allowed to put in a long centreboard or a short one. The short centreboard has an advantage in very strong winds where you have

169

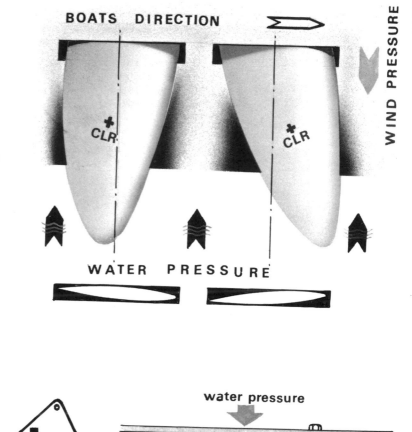

BOATS DIRECTION

WIND PRESSURE

CLR

CLR

WATER PRESSURE

The centre-board can be made to twist to wind-ward by letting it go down a little more.

Or it can be made to angle to windward by shaping the top inside the centre-board case.

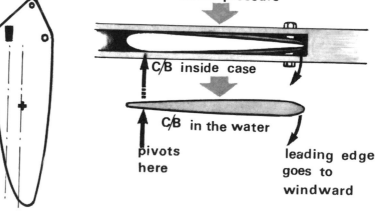

water pressure

C/B inside case

C/B in the water

pivots here

leading edge goes to windward

difficulty in balancing the boat but in light and medium winds the long centreboard will always have the advantage.

Let us discuss now what you must do before a race. Let us take a class I was sailing and in which I really wanted to win—the *Star*.

There you have to tune your boat to the wind condition you are going to expect in that race so in that particular class it is very important to go out in good time and going upwind you tune the mast especially so that the feel on the tiller is light. If you expect very light winds for instance you can, before you go out, move your mast step back and if it is a strong wind you can move it forward to the place where you know approximately it should be.

Then you go out and adjust the position of the sheeting of the jib and finish adjusting the mast. You can adjust the bend with the stays or the wedges or by moving the whole mast so that you feel the boat is lively.

Remember, so many things can happen with a *Star*. A wooden mast can be more dry in drier weather so that it feels stiffer. Also after a strong wind race the sail shape can have altered so you must re-adjust the tuning. The main thing with a *Star* is that after a strong wind race the leach will be more open because it has stretched, and this is very bad in a *Star*. If the sail in a *Star* becomes too open you will never be able to point. If you pull in your sail more to try to be able to point, then the boat stops. With too open a leach you are unable either to point or to get the speed. So it is very important that it is not too open and it is not too closed. Nothing is so sensitive as the leach on a *Star*.

A *Dragon* is the same in one way. There the lower batten has to hook up to windward a bit. Without that you cannot point.

Nobody can tell by looking if a boat is in tune or not. Take me for example. I go out and tune a lot of Finns and other international class boats and maybe think that this boat has a nice feeling, it goes well and so on, but I can't tell you if I am pointing well enough. And I can't tell you in this particular sea if the speed is all right. Even if I could have a flag or an instrument saying that I am pointing well to the wind I am still not sure if I am pointing well enough on a long leg.

For instance in that sea the bow may be moving in such a way so that the result is that I am not really pointing and, therefore, I don't think anyone really can tell exactly if the boat is pointing without testing against a better boat. You can tell whether the boat is balanced right, but you can't tell if you've got the best speed or the best pointing. If one person can feel a boat better than another person then this person must have a great deal of experience or perhaps a special talent.

171

As for me — do I have talent or is it because I have been sailing so much that I have a lot of experience? As a boy I had the feeling that it was both because as a boy I didn't have the experience but I could still do more than the other boys of the same age. But you must have a little talent to be able to tune a boat.

In the preparation of, say, a *Flying Dutchman* or *5-0-5* before a race, I go through everything on the boat to see if everything looks as it should look. Because if a stay looks as if it is going to break or the halliard, the mainsheet, or if a shackle is loose then they must be fixed before the start. Remember something can happen during a race in strong wind and you will first realize it after when you may see that the mast has a crack. If you did not look you might break the mast next time out in only a light wind.

A properly prepared boat ought never to break during a race. It is your own fault if it does break, but some accident during the race can of course do it if you capsize, for example, or perhaps the spinnaker pole could break when you have the spinnaker up and so on. That's something you cannot allow for. In the old days and when I really wanted to be first in a race I went through the boat and I replaced everything where there was a small chance that it might break.

I had not been sitting in a *5-0-5* for eight years and I thought it could be such fun to try to win the World Championship once more. So when I decided to go I bought a Lanaverre *5-0-5* and I first took part in the Australian championships and I found I could not point. So I fixed the centreboard so that I was able to point (see page 169) and I also had different sails with me to test which sails were best on the mast I used. And so I got the boat going and now I felt I had a chance.

We had all morning free because we started racing at twelve or one o'clock. I went through everything on the mast every day to see if it was right. I did well and came second in the World Championship but in the last race I had to finish first to win with Cuneo sixth and Jim Hardy fourth. Hardy went from No. 22 at the first mark up to No. 2 at the finish and so I was very close to winning that World Championship.

Sometimes it is interesting to see that a small accident can tell you that things have to be like so-and-so. For instance when I was sailing with Aage Birch in the *Dragon* Gold Cup in Marstrand we were the only ones to carry a genoa in a very strong wind. We had our lower stays as tight as the upper stays and so with the wind blowing more than 20 metres per second (40 knots) the mast was bending out to the lee side at the top so that we had a bigger distance between the genoa and the mainsail than normal. So the mainsail was therefore flatter and pointing more into the wind. The boat thus had such a light tiller that even in the heaviest gusts it really went fast. But the mast was bending so much that we were afraid to break it, therefore we slacked off the lower stay to make the mast straighter but the boat became immediately slower. So that taught me that when it is blowing tremendously hard it was an advantage with that particular sail to do that. Some years later, I thought I would like to try it with a modern sail to see if it was the same, and I found that from about 13 metres (26 knots) and more it was an advantage to do it but under that wind strength it was a disadvantage.

Another time I sailed a *Dragon* in a wind of 15 metres per second (30 knots) and the mast was bending so much that I was afraid the jumpers would break. Then I received a very hard puff and the jumpers folded right back and the boat became tremendously fast but I was very scared the mast would break. In this case we got the same result from the mast because when the jumpers collapsed the top of the mast went to leeward. At the same time when the mast bent a little forward in the middle the lower stay, which was a little aft of the mast, helped to push the middle of the mast to windward. So in the hardest puff the mast adjusted its sideways bend automatically (see page 162).

In the early days of *Finns* we broke a lot of masts because they collapsed on the aft side near the boom slot and we all realized that just before they broke we were tremendously fast. But we were stupid enough not to take advantage of this at that time. We thought it was a pure accident but later we tried to make it lean aft on purpose. Then Georj Bruder, in Brazil, started making masts which were very soft just above the boom and these masts immediately showed they were much faster than our normal stiff ones. The only thing I can say here is that it was fantastic that it took so many years just to realize the worth of a *Finn* mast which was soft just above the boom.

In the *Snipe* World Championship in '59 in Porto Alegre in the South of Brazil the boats were supplied by the Brazilians. None of us were allowed to come with our own boats, and the boat I drew had a rather stiff mast. In some practice races I had a good speed but in a strong wind I wasn't as fast as I usually was in these conditions. But by accident we had cleated the jib on a dead run with the whisker-pole set and in a hard puff the jib went forward and the pole pushed the mast back so that it broke. After that we got a softer mast which matched our sails better and we then got a tremendous speed in strong winds and were still fast in light and medium winds. So by pure accident we then

173

got a good speed and won the World Championship rather easily.

In the *Finn* Gold Cup in '59 in Copenhagen, my mast half broke in every race and after each race I had to glue some sail battens on the mast to strengthen it but it was still tremendously soft and today I feel that I must have been really stupid not to realize that it was the reason that I had such a good speed in these races.

I crewed for the Danish *5·5-metre* in the World Championship in '61 in Finland, and we had a complex about strong winds and we didn't feel that the boat was really going. There was one race with a very strong wind and towards the end of this race on the last third of the upwind leg, we pulled in the jib sheet and the main sheet much harder than I ever thought that a *5·5-metre* could be sheeted and the boat pointed tremendously high and it had a lovely speed as well. I never forgot that and it shows that it takes such a long time for a man to move from one class to another because the handling and trim is absolutely different from class to class. Here we got a tremendous speed by luck and we managed to get second place overall.

In Norway and Denmark we have a very popular class called the *Knarr-boat* and I once had to tune one in a strong wind. I had made a new sail and it was not really going, so we also took the fastest *Knaar-boat* to tune against. We went out and the boat which I made the new sails for was not pointing or going fast. I pulled in the main and jib to where I thought a *Knaar-boat* should be sheeted but it wasn't until I had been trying everything for twenty minutes that I first realized how slack I should set the main sheet to make the boat really go. And after I had done this I got it to point higher and to go faster than the fastest boat that we were using as pacemaker. So it took twenty minutes for me, and I am used to tuning a lot of different boats, to get the right sheeting position. I felt so stupid that I hadn't been able to find this out earlier and then I remembered how long it takes an average racing man before he finds the right sheeting position and then when the wind changes how long it takes for him to adjust it correctly again.

Nine

Boat handling and tactics

How to win races

Winning a race is very much more than sailing a boat fast. It's taking the opportunity when it comes such as grabbing an overlap at a mark or tacking in exactly the right place so that you put yourself in a better position: all those things. A skipper needs to be quick in his mind, and that's a difficult thing to teach, because one man is intelligent and another is not.

It's quite easy to explain to somebody by words or drawings how the boat should be trimmed, how it should be tuned, how it should be handled; but how it should be raced is another thing altogether.

The qualities needed for winning

The more experience you have, the more you will find that a lot of races have nearly the same situations, but there are so many small variations in races that you forget what you learned last time, and you can make the same mistake again. So let us say that every race is different; that's the reason we never learn. We can never be absolutely sure what we are doing.

An intelligent person who races a great deal can gain a lot of knowledge and experience and improve all the time; but if he can't see exactly how the tide is, and if he can't see exactly where the wind is going to turn and where the wind is strongest, then it is pure luck if his decision is right or wrong. But the experienced skipper will know how to make the best of a bad situation.

Yacht racing is so fascinating because there are so many different things to calculate and to be a successful yachtsman you have to be good in so many different ways. Probably nobody can be perfect in all things and so the really successful skipper is good in most of them, or more than many others.

To be really successful you have to like the boat you are going to

175

race in and you have to like playing with the boat. You have to be prepared to alter anything during the race at any time without taking your eyes away from the racing course and the wind and the sea. All the details of the race you must keep in your head. You have to practise so that everything that can be practised is automatic for you. Then you have time to concentrate on things which are new. All the time you must concentrate on where the wind is going to shift and when the tide is going to change. All the things that you can calculate beforehand must be worked out correctly, and you need a certain intelligence to be able to do all these things and you must like doing them.

I haven't said anything about racing rules or tactics, because that's routine. The racing rules and how they affect the positions between boats—that's something you can work out on shore at any time, and not only during racing.

The Danish pair, Fogh and Petersen, were so well trained that they could "play" with the boat in all conditions.

K. Hashimoto

176

Let us take an example of a standard situation where two or three boats come to the lee mark at the same time, and your boat is one of them. If you are on the lee side of the nearest boat to the mark, you know that if you can't get on to his windward side before you get within two lengths of the mark, then the boat which is coming behind you will be ahead of you when you start going to windward. So you must know automatically that you have to wait and go behind the leading boat, and then tack after the mark, when you are able to tack. That's tactics combined with racing rules and is something you must know before you start racing—it is too late to think about simple tactics like these during the race. What is difficult during a race is to calculate and look where to go, and you need all your thinking energy to do this and so the routine tactics must not take up your time.

Before you start racing seriously you've got to become absolutely familiar with the basic racing rules and the simple tactics.
Take another example—in a start a man tries very hard to start on the line at theoretically the best place, and thinks he will have a big advantage by being exactly there, but he should remember that even though the wind angle may give him an advantage at this place, another boat very close on his lee side may force him to start, maybe half a boat's length late. But what is half a boat's length, as long as he still has free wind and can tack? Nothing. So, working out on paper before the start how much you win or lose in such and such a situation can help you to be quiet and not be nervous in spite of not getting the position you really wanted.

Working out all the possibilities beforehand, you make yourself calm during the race and then you can think much better; this in turn makes the tactics more interesting and the race more fun. In a race, if something happens that you have not prepared for, then something is wrong. You've got to be ready for everything.

Another example, where they set out the course wrongly and the boats can lay the first mark. Very good people sometimes tack just after the start automatically, even though they could have laid the mark, and it means that they were starting without knowing where to go. What a big mistake, and yet it often happens. You should never make any mistakes where you are able to see or calculate what will happen.

On the other hand I can remember that once we were sailing close along the shore and there was very little wind and the tide was against us. We continued along the shore until we dared go out across the tide to the mark. But by the time that we dared go out, another boat had already started on the way, but much too early, and then the wind

177

suddenly came and saved him. It was pure luck that he got enough wind to get round. He took a risk, but that was luck, and that's all. That's a part of the game. You can't say that the man was clever — he just took the chance. No, maybe you can say he was clever, because he might have said, "If I had stayed behind the others along the shore, I am sure I would never have passed them. So I took the chance and hoped for the wind to come." So in that way, he was clever to take the chance if it was vital for him to be the winning boat. If the race was for a prize on its own, he would only want to win, but if it was one of a series, perhaps a lower place, but a safe one, would be enough.

The advice that I would give to a keen young skipper starting international racing is that he must always remember, however hard it is to accept, that the winner almost never wins through luck; there is always a reason for it. He must realize that he could do it, too, if he knew enough about it. It is something he can learn. There is always a reason why these experts always seem to be able to go from the back to the front so easily. One good reason is that they are sailing faster than the others and it is so easy to win if you have tuned your boat better. You don't need much tactical knowledge to do that. But sometimes someone comes up to the front in a shifty wind, with a boat which is quite slow. There are a lot of these people and they win in these conditions because they handle their boats better, they can tack without losing anything, they tack in the right places and they go the right way. These people are clever and we know a lot of them.

Once I was invited to race on a lake near Bordeaux in a borrowed *Finn*. I was very scared because they had invited me and paid my aeroplane ticket and I was afraid that I would not show them my best, but fortunately I won. But in one race I remember there was very little wind and there was an advantage in being at the starboard end of the line, so all the boats were there. But it was a light shifty wind and so I was standing up in the *Finn* and watching where the wind came from and I saw a wind shift of 90° coming and this changed the advantage so that we should start at the other end. So I immediately sailed right down to the other end and the line was very long and nobody followed me. I was alone, and just after the start the wind changed — bang! — and I was far away from the rest of the fleet. I think I won by ten minutes. And so again, if there is something you can see, you must see it. That was wonderful, because it was not luck, but many people still thought I was lucky.

The start is the most important thing. If you get a good start it is half the race, and a good start takes more than that — it takes the most

out of a man. The start needs concentration and thought. I have to work
very hard to make a start where I can be certain I am going to succeed.
I only do it if it is important that I want to win that race. If I don't like to
win that race but I just want to sail then I never calculate anything.
I am just playing. But if I really want to make a good start then it is very
hard work for me.

Sometimes when there have been six general recalls and ahead of
that general recall you have been one hour on the course and practised
everything, then that race doesn't interest me at all because the committee has not done a proper job. Firstly, they are not starting at the right
time and then they start general recalls even though only two or three
boats are over the line, instead of calling them back. Then this race
means nothing to me. Because I have lost concentration.

When I start I try to keep clear water to windward so that I can
tack, and clear water to leeward of course if I want to get the speed on
the same tack, and in this case if I see someone wanting to bear off and
go on to my lee side, I bear off and try to get them onto my windward
side. I prefer to have them on the windward side if I want to continue on
starboard.

But if I want to tack immediately then I will do everything I can to
get them to go on my lee side, and if I want to tack I try to start near the
starboard end of the line.

There is a simple method of finding with great accuracy which is
the favoured end of the starting line. One sails along the line with the
sheets eased until they are flapping almost completely but with very
slight tension on the main sheet. Then, keeping the sheet cleated at
this position you tack the boat and exactly reverse your course by
pointing at the other mark. If the mainsail then fills even slightly more,
the port end is favoured and vice versa.

Paul would have none of this. He maintained that putting the
boat head to wind and glancing sideways abeam was good enough.
This is certainly not accurate for most people who regard a few yards'
advantage to windward at the start as being worth a great deal. Paul
disagreed. It is far more important which way you go. If you cannot tack
after the start you can easily lose fifty metres which can be far more
than you might gain by being at the more windward end of the line.

The most important thing is to be free on your windward side so
that you can tack. Do everything you can to encourage boats approach-
ing from astern to pass you before the start. If the port end is favoured,

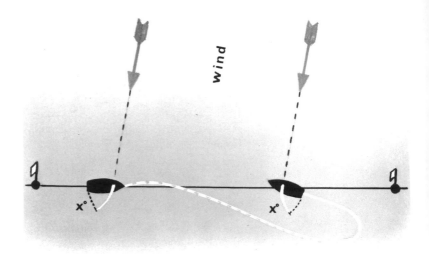

then a tactic Paul frequently uses is to time himself to arrive at the lee mark with the gun. Then he is in complete command since his back-wind and the waves from his speeding boat spoil all those to windward and behind. He can very soon tack and rub in his mastery of the situation by crossing the fleet. But this tactic needs constant practice and absolute accuracy of timing.

Starting tactics

Paul. I can always remember the races where the others made mistakes and where I did not. For instance, there was one race in the pre-Olympics at Acapulco where I practised starting on starboard tack and watched the wind and then I tried port tack and also watched the wind. I found that it did not matter where I started since the mean wind was about at right angles to the line even though the wind was shifting a lot from time to time. But one minute before the start the wind changed from the mean to the side which gave the port end the advantage. So nearly everyone rushed down that end but the important thing with that sort of wind is that you should start at the port end and tack and then continue on port tack until the wind goes back not to the mean direction but to past the mean wind.

Ninety per cent of the fleet started down at the port end of the line and I started in the middle, but that was fun because I started and tacked. The others lost because they could not tack on to port whereas I could tack immediately. The others had to wait until the windward

180

boats tacked and I was gaining all the time they waited. So when I got the windshift back again I tacked and passed all of them. It was only one-and-a-half or two minutes after the start, so fast can the wind change.

Starting in "coffin corner"

In the Naples Olympics there was no inner distance mark at the Committee boat end and so the people who came under its stern to start would never be able to get up into that triangle. So there I came down from the wrong side of the line on port tack, went down and tacked in the last fifteen seconds and got a splendid start. In the

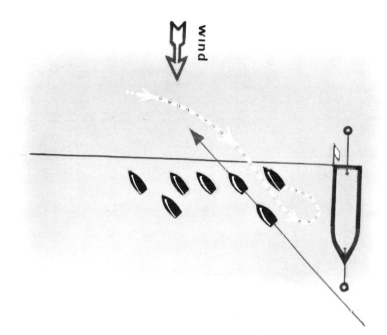

Olympics everybody is so nervous about being put out that they are less likely to try that than they would in any other sort of racing. But if there are other people who want to come in there then you have to decide what to do. But the more practice and training you have had in your boat the more precise you can be because you know exactly how your boat will behave, how you can control it, how you can stop it, how close you can go, how to start again. The cleverer you are with this balance between the mainsheet, the tiller, the jib sheet your crew and everything, the more precisely you can make a start.

181

If there are too many boats and the tide is against us, my own experience is that they all start too late. So I start on the weather side of the line then and dive back just before the gun. If the tide is with us they will have general recall after general recall and they'll never start. It is hopeless and the only thing you can do is to be with the leading group and hope for the best.

If you are the only boat to keep behind the line you cannot win. Remember when you think you are on the line and there are twenty boats over the line you cannot say where the line is because you cannot see it, so it is better to be protected so that the committee cannot see you and then you are still alive if they let the start go. But I don't like to speak about such starts because that's very bad for yacht racing when it happens. When the tide is against you you can come from the wrong side of the line and go down behind the line. You will find a hole because the tide is against you. I have the experience that when the tide is so strong other boats will be far from the line.

To tell when you are on the line you can take a bearing on the shore or something else. I try to do that but it is better that you concentrate where the mark is and keep it in your mind all the time. If the tide is against you and you can keep on the line then it is very important that you stay on the line all the time. If I am starting in the middle of the line my experience is that if I think I am half a boat's length over the line then I am exactly on the line.

You must be on the right windshift absolutely from the start so that if you have to go onto port tack after the start because of the wind you must put your boat in a position so that you are able to tack. It is so important that you put yourself in a position so that you are able to tack when you ought to tack otherwise you can find yourself continuing and continuing on the wrong tack. I have a big handicap in that people are following me thinking that I go the right way and I often can't tack because they are there.

I was surprised to find that Paul did not use a compass much when racing. He said that he used one in the *5·5-metre* and the *Star* but only to find the weather mark. The Committee can give you the compass course to the mark and you can then check it against landmarks.

Paul admitted that there was much more that he could have done to prepare himself and his boat for racing and the use of compasses was one of the ways he was intending to improve in the future.

I mentioned the pre-Olympic regatta at Acapulco when most of the *Finn* fleet got lost and sailed for the wrong mark. Paul had rounded the previous mark nearly last, realized the fleet was in error, went for the right mark and won the race. Paul denied that a compass would have helped him there had he been ahead since he insisted that he would have remembered where he had come from.

This constant checking of bearings both ahead and astern was frequently referred to in our conversations. He mentioned it in connection with checking wind shifts after the start when, if he was ahead and with a clear horizon, the only bearings he had were his own course relative to those astern.

However, he finally said that in his "older days" he was going to use a compass!

Paul. If you are out on the open sea and you have no land marks to guide you then I think a compass, if you know how to use it, will help a lot. But you can always look back to check your angle on the other boats and the starting marks. I can see a windshift or a gust if the sun is not against me because the sun makes a pattern on the water. But when the sun is shining in a way so that you can't see the windshift on the water, then I am sailing like a blind man. You have to watch the windshifts on the water.

In the last *5·5-metre* World Championship that I won in Copenhagen I really wanted to win because that was my only chance ever to win it and I went out one hour before every start. As soon as I knew about where the line would be I put my boat on to starboard and was sailing and sailing and sailing so that I knew the highest and lowest direction of the wind as it shifted back and forth. I did not use a compass—I just watched. We had mainly wind from the shore and because I live there it was easy for me to recognize the direction.

So when we started I could see immediately if I was on the mean direction or was pointing too low or very high. If I had been in a foreign place it would have been more difficult because I could not have remembered that point, or that point. I have never learnt to use a compass but I would say I am going to do it. I am going to learn but I think that if you have not learnt to use a compass, if you don't have the technique of using it, then it can be worse.

We had the wind from the shore in this championship, and it was very shifty, but I never made a mistake because I was so prepared before the start. I said, "Now you are too low—Tack!" and we tacked

183

and continued pointing very high to the next shift. When I tacked on the next course I knew directly that if I could lay that point I was on the high course and when I came lower than Vedbaek harbour, that was the mean—a little lower, and then I must tack again.

I remember for instance in one race that I came from behind up to Sundelin of Sweden, who later won in Acapulco, I was faster than him, a little faster all the time, and when I had nearly passed him and could give him very bad wind I saw that we had gone the wrong way and so I tacked immediately. But he was happy that I had tacked and so he continued. But the next time we met I was far ahead. And so that's an example of a situation where you should not race against the people who are closest to you. In shifty wind you are racing against the wind. Look at the mark in the distance. Think of the mark always. How to come fastest to that mark.

I had a tremendous battle at Copenhagen in the '59 *Finn* Gold Cup in one race with André Nelis of Belgium when the wind was very shifty. I should have won that particular race but we had a misunderstanding. I tacked on to starboard near the finish and because I tacked close I did not ask for water so I was going under his stern. But then he tacked because he suddenly saw me on starboard. There was no protest

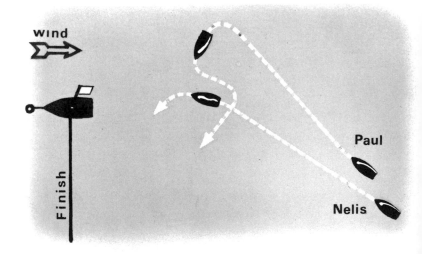

or anything. We only misunderstood each other. We were both too careful. Because of this I had to bear even more away and I lost a lot of ground just before the finish line. I had been behind and came closer and closer but he was clever with the windshifts and was not trying to cover me. He was too clever to pass because he tacked to follow the wind, and he made it very difficult for me because he didn't make any mistakes. It was very difficult for me just to keep near him. And then he made some small mistake just before the finish line and I came up close and had a chance to win. But our misunderstanding meant that I did not win. But I did not mind—it was such a good race.

In a shifty wind you have to sail after the wind and the boat behind you will mainly do the opposite and so he will do the wrong thing all the time. On the other hand, quite often, if you have a man ahead of you that you are trying to catch you can tack on the wind shifts and he will always be too late. He will be later all the time and you will come closer and closer. The closer you get the more anxious he gets and the more he loses. You can work on a man's nerves like this. Get him really worked up so that every time he covers too quickly and stops the boat and so you come closer still. And at the last minute you are overtaking him so fast that you are past and away.

I can normally tell beforehand if the gust will lift me or will head me, but it depends what side of the gust I am on because a gust fans out; generally speaking, if the whole gust has the mean direction then it fans out and you are lifted if you are on the lee side of the gust and headed if you are on the windward side.

You have got to know where you are in a gust. Whether you are on the lee side or the weather side of it, because that governs your tactics. You may want to sail on into the gust or you may want to tack immediately. But it also depends what is behind that gust. Because if the sun is at such an angle that you can easily see the gust far away you may be able to see that there is no wind behind it—there is a hole. Perhaps there is a lot of wind over there and so it is better to bear away and get through that gust even though you can't point and then you take the next gust and maybe tack and follow that for a long time. And so you get round behind the hole.

In strong wind when the sun is good—that is the easiest weather to see the wind. Even in rough water you can see the gusts coming but it depends on the sun. Even if there is no sun, that could be very good. It depends where the light comes from. I would say that even for me it is mainly quite difficult to see the wind but when you are able to see the windshifts on the water then you must take the advantage. It is not normally unlucky to sail into holes. You can always see where the wind is on the water. But you sometimes need luck because you can see something on the water but what comes behind that, you don't know.

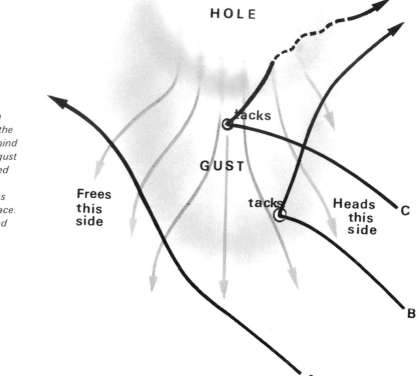

HOLE

tacks

GUST

Frees
this
side

tacks

Heads
this
side   C

B

A

Here is a diagram of a fairly typical gust on the water with a hole behind it. A, who meets the gust on the left side, is freed and then headed but should not tack. B has tacked in the right place. C has gone too far and falls into the hole.

Cutting your
losses

When you fight just before the finish line against another person and you go in opposite directions and nobody can see what wind you will receive, then you need luck. Even in close quarter battles, where there are boats all around, you have got to try to look outside the group. You must try to see where the wind is even in the heat of battle. The worst thing is to be near another boat which can forbid you to tack in shifty winds. If you get caught the wrong side of the shift or it looks as though things are going wrong you must cut your losses and get away to the side that you know is right. You mustn't stay on the same tack that you know is getting worse and worse. You have to realize and accept that you have lost so much and hope that the others will make a mistake later.

You must work out what is the right thing to do and then try to work up again and hope something will happen later, because the race is never finished before the line is crossed. It could make the race very interesting for you by saying, "O.K. I have lost here. Bad luck. I could not avoid it. Let me try to get it right from now on". Then you try to see how far up you can get. It is a much better race for you to come from number 50 to number 10 than for the chap who has been leading all the way who then loses the first place on the line and becomes second. You feel much better than him.

Attacking on a reach

We talked about tactics you can employ on a reach or a run to catch a boat ahead. You can, for example, luff very slowly when the skipper ahead is not looking and then when he sees you he will often alter course more suddenly and lose a yard or two. Then you bear away slowly and he again follows more suddenly, losing another few yards and so on.

But Paul said he had never used this technique which seemed to me surprising since I considered it basic and almost elementary. But he said that he was used to sailing in big fleets and, for boats which are basically able to travel only at identical speeds one can only lose on the leaders by such tactics. He preferred to encourage the boat ahead to sail straight on as fast as possible and then to try to pass him on the next upwind leg. By this means he said that one did not lose on the leaders. Always at the top of his priorities is the need to win the race—not just to pass a few boats which is maybe the top ambition of lesser mortals. A good placing is not in his reckoning—it has to be a win!

Luffing

Again, on luffing he prefers not to place himself in a position where he can be taken off for a ride. This is more likely in a keelboat class where an injudicious poking of one's nose past the weather quarter of the next ahead could result in a costly detour to windward. In a dinghy such a situation can be retrieved at a late stage by a violent zig-zag to reduce speed and a dive under the leader's stern to a safe lee position.

Paul. Let us say that you round the lee mark and you cannot quite get an overlap and then you are going to harden up on to the wind and you are dead behind the chap ahead. Perhaps one boat's length behind. If it is such a big disadvantage to tack then you have to stay behind the boat ahead but if he is the leader then I will be away under his lee side and continue there. Normally you have to be very close to him to do that otherwise you lose a lot of distance to leeward. It depends on your speed. If I am a little faster than him then I go to lee. If I am slower than him then I will stay behind him to make sure I stay ahead of the next boat. But if there are two boats in front of me I will stay behind because if I bear away I have to be very fast.

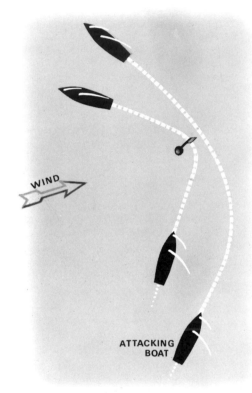

To prepare for the rounding I will bear away before the mark and then go up to a reach and stay on a reach because then I will pass the mark with full speed. Then I try to go straight through his lee and then luff, but never pointing too high until I am ahead of him.

You have to get through his wind shadow. You must keep the speed and so you must put the traveller and everything to lee. It is not important to point at all because you have to get so far forward that he gives up trying to bear away. If he starts to bear away then the boat behind can gain a lot by pointing high and you cannot tack to cover.

You have to think also how far there is to the next mark and what
the tide is doing. If the tide is less to leeward then you are not losing
much because then you go into less tide and you have a long way to
go to the mark. But you don't have to decide what to do until the last
minute. It depends on what the leading boat is going to do. Your crew
must be well trained.

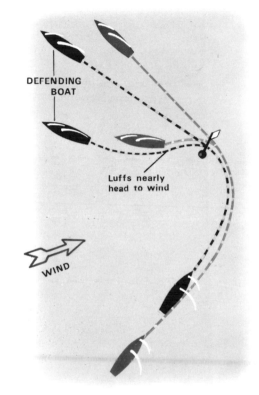

DEFENDING
BOAT

Luffs nearly
head to wind

WIND

It is a help to know your competitor ahead. Let us say that he is
the type who is never pointing high but he always bears away and
sails free. Then I would bear away before the mark and go very close
to the mark and start pointing and hope to get clear air on the windward
side.

Now, equally, if you are ahead and you want to stop a man coming
through from behind you have got to be very quick as you go round that
mark. If he is going to carry on pointing the best thing to do is to luff a
little bit as you round and you put him straight behind you in your

backwind, but you have got to watch all the time that he doesn't bear away at full speed under your lee.

In the Olympics in 1968, in the first race in the *Star,* I was first and Lowell North of U.S.A. was second and Peder Lunde of Norway, third. When I turned the mark I could see that North wanted to go down to my lee side. So I did not point at all and I was spoiling him so much that he lost an enormous amount. Peder Lunde was just behind but I was not afraid of him. You see, it was in the first race and so I didn't then realize his good speed.

North was so far behind that he was behind Lunde, but by then he was very far down to leeward—about fifty metres—before he got a clear wind. And then he went like a steamer and he was so far away that I could never affect him with my wind shadow. He came through, pointed and went up ahead of me. He was a little lucky with the wind but all the same he was much faster than me so that his gain was enormous.

That was an example where I watched him to try to spoil him as much as I could. I tried to get the biggest distance between us and I did it, but my speed was too bad. But I delayed him passing me by fifteen minutes, and who knows what might have happened in that time. And so I mean that if I had been a little faster with my boat speed I would have been a sure winner.

You have to know the racing rules so that you are absolutely sure that what you do is right. With port and starboard, for example, you always know whether you are right or wrong. But it becomes much more difficult to know what to do when you get complex situations with several boats going round marks, for example, and this is where you have to study really hard I think. But when you are racing three or four *Finns* all the winter and summer every day you get these situations happening and then if you teach your friends these rules, then you remember them better yourself. Therefore, you should always try to gather three or four people, or more if you can, whom you can race against always, so that you know each other and you all learn the rules together.

I found that some of my friends were not interested in the rules at all but were only interested in sailing fast and I tell you that was a weak point in their career as international dinghy sailors. They were not clever enough in the rules so they were not making the right tactics.

I remember Helmar Petersen once said to me, "I'm satisfied being behind you as long as you don't do something to disqualify me". It was when we were together racing in Kiel Week and he had a complex that at home I could always do something to put him in a bad position, and one of the reasons was that he was not clear enough in the rules. So to be able really to win you must know the rules in order to be able to calculate the tactics. When you read the rules you should think of the tactics at the same time.

In the early days of the *5-0-5s* in La Baule during the World Championship, once we were practising the start and we found we could lay the first mark. Therefore, we must never put ourselves in a position at the start where we had to tack after the gun, but at the same time, there was such a great advantage in being at the starboard mark, and we knew that there would come so many beginners from upwind bearing down to try to get room at the mark. I was prepared for that and the one bad thing that could happen was that one boat could come down and pass us and stay there to windward. Maybe he would not realize that he would be too early so I told Pierre, my crew, to call out in French that they won't get room. They must read the rules. Pierre did this and at the same time I said to him, "If someone comes down and touches us don't push them back but take your right hand and just keep them back". Because if he pushed them back it pushed us forward and we would be over the line. I mean they broke the rules first by touching us and so we did this. O.K. you can say we broke the rules or not as you like, but you must try to get the best out of any situation. You must be practical.

Sailors are better on the rules today than they were in the early days, but I must say, when too many boats are starting, it is not really nice but it's not the fault of the skippers—it's the fault of starting too many boats. When there are too many boats they can't see where the line is or anything, and that makes people break the rules. It is only natural for people to do that.

I sometimes meet a chap who gets into a boat and doesn't seem to be trying and I have a tremendous work beating him in one or two races. Then in other races he was *far* behind. I was always thinking if this chap really had been training—had been living his whole life for being first in racing—would he by nature have had a bigger talent than me? But then today when I look back I have been thinking of these people and it seems that in these particular races they have had luck to find a better tuning and that was the main reason for their success.

There could be many reasons for the British *Flying Dutchman* in Acapulco being so fast but most of all I think it was their very good teamwork and that was because of their training. Remember that with the genoa, the main, and the spinnaker up at the same time there is a

191

But even though you have tuned your boat to be balanced you still cannot be sure that you have maximum speed. You must not then say that neutral helm is wrong and that maybe your boat goes faster with weather helm. When a boat is in balance maybe you will find that you are not pointing but that is because of your sail. When the boat is well balanced you feel the boat goes fast even though you may be bearing off and it goes nicely whatever you do. Therefore, you have to concentrate very precisely to be able to point. But if you can do it then the boat will be fastest.

A little weather helm can give a good result but generally speaking it should be so little that it is better to say that it balances exactly. In medium winds you should be able to hold the tiller with one finger and if it is too much to hold with one finger then it is too much weather helm. You should also be able to steer to windward with one finger in strong winds but, nevertheless, in a strong wind you would, in practice, grip the tiller very hard, and make the boat go where you want it to. But the boat must be in balance because if it has a weather helm, and because of the sea you want to bear off for instance, you will stop the whole boat. You will have to put on too much helm and then you put on the brakes. When you steer the boat sometimes you will be luffing and sometimes you will bear off. The helm balance must be neutral and then you can steer the boat and the rudder is never stopping the boat. But in general it is more important that the sail has the right angle to the wind and that the boat has the right angle to the sea.

In a very light wind you can adjust the sail very finely when there is very little sea because the boat is not being knocked about. You can pull the boom down quite a long way so that the leach is very straight because you can keep an accurate course. But in a strong wind where the boat is being knocked about a lot it's an advantage to ease the sail to get rather more twist into it because then at least some of the sail will be working all the time. A *5·5-metre* or *Soling* you can always steer precisely but other boats you cannot. With those boats which you can't keep precisely, you have to ease off the sheets.

In a keelboat the amount that you need to move the sheet or the traveller could be very, very small indeed to make a big difference. When I was sailing a *Star* we had marks on the sheet and we found that about an inch on that sheet seemed to make a difference. In a boat like a *Star* the boom is very close to the deck, and if you tighten the mainsheet it is exactly the same as tightening the leach more or less. And that is very important.

194

Therefore, if you are sailing the boat to windward with the traveller out you will have to have quite a tight leach in order to point and then a very small difference on the sheet will also make quite a big difference to killing the boat or to getting it moving. But if you are sailing in rough seas where you have got the boom in and up a bit to give twist to the sail, then the exact tension is not quite so critical.

In the case of the *Star,* if the mainsail leach is made to "open" then you have to pull in the mainsheet more to "close" it so that you can point, and then the whole leach becomes too tight and the boat stops. Therefore, it is very important in strong winds that the *Star* leach is made so that it is "closed" because then you don't have to pull in the mainsheet too much to be able to point. I mean that you can ease the mainsheet and still have the mainsail in the right shape for pointing. Also in strong winds you must not ease the mainsheet in a *Star* or it will get lee helm. So again you shall make the sail with a "closed" leach. I mean, it is no good going out with a sail of the wrong cut in some types of boat, especially a *Star.*

When I go to another new racing place, I take a lot of trouble to find out the tide pattern and the wind pattern and what the weather is likely to do. But it is mainly experience which tells me what will happen. In Meulan on the Seine I was sailing with Strit in a twenty-four hour race and we came third. It was the most flukey place to race but I was often there and realized that there was a sense in it because the same people won. Therefore I told myself I had to learn it. Then I came back in a *5-0-5* and I won. And then in a *Finn* I won too because now I was knowing the water. I always profited very much from experience. If I was beaten somewhere I worked it out afterwards and puzzled over it. I don't like to put it down to good luck and bad luck.

It's the same at the Ski-yachting Regatta at Cannes in January because it has the most hopeless weather you can receive, but year after year I go there and there are some main rules that you have to follow to have a reasonable chance.

If my speed is slower than the others O.K. that's accepted, there is nothing I can do if I can't find a better speed in a hurry, but if my speed is just as good as yours then it is up to me to place my boat in the right place. It was from my experience in Meulan and Cannes that I changed myself from a hard wind sailor to also a good light wind skipper. I used to be so bad in light winds, and I worked and worked and worked at it and yet I hated it to start with because I wanted to win. Today, I say the more shifts there are in the wind the more interesting it is because in a steady wind you can only win by boat speed. When the

195

wind is changing and there are difficult conditions you can win by doing the right things. This kind of racing today I find more interesting.

When I first came to Cowes I heard it was a place where there were more interesting things happening, shall we put it, than anywhere else in the world. You have got wind and tide going round in circles and up and down, but I also remember the choppy sea. It was rough and I found it was something new to work with. I liked that, but in the last race there we had no wind at all and the tide was strong. We went along the shore and I was leading by a long distance and then came the wind from offshore. The boats which were out in the sea came up and we couldn't get out to the wind. Then the race was cancelled. But I didn't like that — at Cowes, there must be wind. Where there's a place with tide there must be wind and then it is fun. But with no wind it's not fun.

I remember when I was sailing with Richard and Augusta Creagh-Osborne in their *X-boat,* there was no wind and we got swept out through the Needles' channel. That's not fun, but Richard told me that was the *only* race in eight years that had ever happened. I don't know what I did to the wind that day but it is always the same story. When I went to Seattle my friends there said it was the only day they had seen snow in three years. How many times have I been to places and they say, "Oh, it never normally does this". Do you know in the Olympic Games it is always abnormal weather!

I find that the more the wind shifts, the more interesting it is because if I lose, for instance, I have the chance to come up again. But in a steady wind it is mainly the speed that matters. The tactics are more interesting in changing winds and difficult conditions. But on the other hand, it's not fun to race when your boat is slower than others and so a new owner must first of all learn the handling of his new boat and when he can handle it he must then learn to tune the boat and for that he must get help. It is faster for him if he gets help from someone in the same class.

Handling, steering a boat, adjusting the sheets and learning to know the boat better and better so that you know exactly what happens if you do so and so, you can only do if you go out sailing on your own. When we come to tuning the boat you have to go exactly by what other people say. You can never be sure that what the best people do is the fastest. Maybe other combinations can be faster. But you can copy what is the fastest tuning today and from there you can make up your mind if you can find something better. In general the fundamental rule is that the fastest is right and the slowest wrong.

"The cleverer you are
with the balance between
mainsheet, tiller, jib-
sheet, your crew and
everything, the more
precisely you can make a
start."

There are
many fast
combinations

There are many ways of tuning a boat to make it go faster
because you find people winning races with bending masts and others
with stiff masts, for example, and you find people winning races with a
lot of twist in the mainsail and some with the mainsail flat. This is
because there are a thousand combinations that can have nearly the
same speed. But sometimes some people find a fantastic speed and then
we must look carefully at that combination and copy it and from there
maybe we can continue to develop the tuning.

But sometimes good tuning is something we can't measure.
We have found when we have tried to copy the tuning of fast boats that

197

we can never get the same speed whatever we do. So it's not always easy, but that makes it interesting.

Some of us sometimes get a tremendous speed upwind or downwind and we can't really tell why. It just happens.

For instance, let us take my old Lanaverre *Finn*. Never mind who was sitting in that boat it planed so much faster than any other *Finn*. Even at 60° to the wind it had such a tremendous speed. Later we found that a *Finn* had to be stiff and yet this Lanaverre was so soft. We can only guess why it was so fast on planing but we don't really know the main reason. And when I had it and was planing people thought that I was clever. I was not clever at all. It just went fast on its own.

It is hard to win with a slow boat

On the other hand I was crewing as tactician for William Berntsen in the *5·5-metre* World Championship in Finland and there we were definitely slower than the first fifteen people but we managed to be second overall. It was quite interesting that for me it was an easy and instinctive feeling which was the way I should go. In these five or six races I only made one mistake, and that was in the last race where the wind came from the sea and I had not seen it. I calculated wrongly and maybe I should have been able to see it but I failed. In the other races I did not make any tactical mistakes but our speed was too slow so we finished second.

Again, in the *Flying Dutchman* World Championship in St. Petersberg, Florida, we were definitely slower. I don't really know the reason why we were so slow but it's a fact that we were slow. I think it was because of four or five different things all together but I can say that we never made any tactical mistakes and so we were able to win.

There was another competitor who had a tremendous speed and he came to me after the first race and said, "There you were lucky" and I told him why we had won because it was not right to say that. Then I said, "I think you were stupid that with such a speed you were not able to win" — only because it was bad sportsmanship not to say "Congratulations, well done".

We had in particular one very hard wind race. I had all the sweaters I could wear and I used the low trapeze position and I was so heavy. When you are on the low trapeze you go first down and then you go straight out, and I used to have strong legs but I nearly couldn't get out, so heavy was I. But even though I was so heavy we were still not the fastest boat but we went the right way and won the race. We became slower and slower, race after race. It is something that happens in yachting — where you don't really know what is wrong. I think it was a

198

combination of so many things but we were so confused that the only thing we could do was to throw the whole boat away and try again.

Winning big
races is difficult

Of course, what it comes to really is that winning big races is difficult and you have got to have a lot of knowledge and experience unless you are lucky. You can't expect to pick up exactly the way to win races from a book or from talking to somebody. Every little thing that you can pick up from a book or person all helps towards it if you can understand it. Open your mind to all the ideas that you can try.

I have been thinking that maybe it's not so important for some people to win a race. Maybe it's more important for these people just to know *how* to win a race. The main thing is that we all enjoy competing in a race, and I am definitely sure that there are a lot of people who like to know what they should do to win a race but they are not so interested in actually trying hard enough to be able to win. They are more interested in competing and playing with friends, and getting contact with other people and having a nice time in the club after the race and talking about the race. People who are winning must remember that they are not necessarily better than the people they beat but the people who win are just more interested in winning.

This story of Paul's, of course, is an object lesson in how you can enjoy racing as well as win big races. Paul started by having tremendous determination to win for a number of years but then he suddenly realized that he was missing something. He was going at it too hard. Today, because of his tremendous store of experience he still can't help winning more often than not, but he enjoys himself. But a lot of people who may have realized how important it is to enjoy themselves a good deal earlier in their racing life, may never really win, but they can still have fun.

But I am sure that everybody who races wants to feel that he has got a chance of winning, even a very slim chance, otherwise he wouldn't really do it.

Paul. We all race in classes where there are many people like this. They want to feel that they have got a chance but they are often worried about the boat and they normally think it is the boat that is slow. They never really admit to themselves that it is they who are slow, even though the top skippers are continually reassuring them about their

199

boats. In many cases their boats are not as fast as the others and then, of course, it is the boat.

You have to be very clever to beat a person who has a fast boat. On the other hand the chap who has the fast boat must be very stupid to lose. But most people have a boat which is not faster than the others and, of course, then they are blaming the boat and maybe it helps themselves to continue racing. They like sailing and they believe that what they do is right so they enjoy it because of the feeling that it is the boat which is wrong.

I never did anything special to my *Finn* because I was one hundred per cent thinking of the Olympic Games. The other races didn't interest me at all at that time except of course for the tactics. I often changed boats to be able to practise getting into the new boat to get it going because I knew that in the Olympics I wouldn't have my own boat and I think that was one of the main reasons I have been good in the Olympics. I have been used to going down into a new boat and then to get it tuned. In the Olympic Games you have seen, sometimes, that people who have been very good in their own boats have been very bad in the Olympics, mainly because their own *Finn* was so fast. But I think that I have been better in the Olympics than in other races.

Ten

Thoughts on the past and the future

My weaker side

Most clever helmsmen have a weak side. My weak side has changed from year to year. When I was a young man, racing in a light wind was my weakest side, because I was not intelligent enough to calculate where the wind would go and I didn't use my eyes well enough in the lighter stuff. In other words, I was mainly concentrating on boat speed in medium and strong winds, and tactics using the wind didn't interest me enough.

Then when I realized that I should use my eyes more to see the wind I became a rather good light wind sailor too. After about 1960 I had really no weak side except that today I am rather lazy. I don't look carefully at the programme now unless it is absolutely necessary and I don't concentrate enough before the start because this is the hardest work of all.

Starting the race is the hardest part

If I really want to be the best in a start, I have to work so hard that it's not fun, and therefore today my weak side is that I don't take the result of racing as seriously as I used to, and that's the main reason I feel I don't do so well as I could do. Today, just to be on the water and to play in a race with good friends I feel is so important that I have become not so good as I was as a top racing man.

My problem at the Olympics in 1968 was that I was not prepared enough. I thought it would be very light winds like the year before so I was not tuning the boat for a wind *at all*. I know I was not fast in the wind that we got but I never expected it and, therefore, I was not thinking of working hard to keep the boat going in all conditions. My mind was fixed only on light winds and maybe I was a little too careless really.

201

We were not allowed to alter anything during the racing because they would not measure us again after the start of the first race. That was a big handicap because I was not able to tune the boat before Acapulco because we had no competition. I was going to tune in the practice races and the first points races but I had an accident with the rig and I broke two stays and so I first met the others in the first points race and then I could alter nothing because the boat was already measured. But it was my own fault. I was not prepared enough so I accepted as it was and enjoyed the time, that's all.

I think a few years ago when I was very hard racing in *Finns* I always covered every possibility, but this time I was not going to the Olympics to win. I was going to the Olympics to enjoy myself and I was scared to be too prepared in case I got my old nerves back. In order to be absolutely sure you have got to take a *lot* of trouble to get the boat prepared so that you are tuned for all conditions. I don't know why but I was really lazy for this Olympics and it didn't interest me so much to win. If I should be prepared to win I ought to have a new rig so that I

could get better tuning in medium and strong winds. It didn't interest me because I am alone in Denmark and I had no one to tune with. My speed was too bad.

A fundamental principle that I began to use later on in international racing, world championships, Gold Cup and so on, was to sail steadily and quietly. If I am not doing anything risky, then in points races I feel that I will always finish at the top end of the fleet and that's the reason I was quiet in the *5-0-5* in Adelaide and in the *5·5-metre* World Championships and the last two *Star-boat* "Worlds" in '66 and '67.

In the last World Championship in the *Star-boat* class which I won in Copenhagen, I was really having bad luck but I was calm in my mind and I had a good place all the time. In the last race I had to be 15 boats ahead of North and about 10 boats ahead of Pinegin of Russia in order to win, and so I never expected to win. Really the main thing for me was that I was happy if all the foreigners visiting my waters were happy.

And then in that last race I managed to get 17 places ahead of North and 20 places ahead of Pinegin so I won the World Championship without expecting it at all. So this shows that when you are a steady sailor you will always be in a good place.

In that series I had the same speed as most people. I was not faster but I was steady. You can say I had a good stroke of luck because in that last race my two closest competitors by chance did so badly but you can turn it up and say that in some other races I had bad luck. So today I just sail steadily and I know in a points race that I will always finish in a good place because of that.

The Olympic Classes

I have competed in all the Olympics since 1948, except in Tokyo where I was spare man because of my nerves so I know a lot about it but today I don't want to give an opinion of what classes we should have in the Olympics. It is a matter of policy because if we say that in the Olympics we should have classes which could help yachting to grow or help yachting to be even more popular than it is today, then I think we have to take the most popular classes. But if we say the Olympics should only be for the best yachtsmen in the world, physically and technically and tactically, then we must have very light boats which have tremendous speeds and of course they will be very difficult to sail and quite expensive.

If anybody asked me what classes I would prefer, I would not like to take part in that discussion because when I was a young man I would have said that the Olympics should only be for the specialist, but today I am leaning more towards anything that can help yachting to grow and so then we should choose the more popular classes. But I cannot forget the feelings I had when I was young and therefore I would like to support the way all young people are thinking today and so I would prefer not to propose anything like that.

The dinghies

Let us look at the Olympic classes today. The *Finn* has been perfect in all Olympics and seems really to be an Olympic boat. With the *Finn* you win because of good tactics and fair racing. We know today that the *Flying Dutchman* needs almost too much luck to get the tuning right and when you get it right the difference in speed between the boats is so big that the racing is not amusing. Therefore, I still say as I have always said that the *5-0-5* has more amusing racing because the speed between different *5-0-5s* is much closer and we know that no-one has been able to tune a *5-0-5* so that it is so much faster than others. The boat and the tuning in the *Flying Dutchman* class seems to be so important that I find it is not a boat for the Olympics. Olympic boats firstly must be cheap and secondly the difference between the boats must be very small.

The keelboats

I think the *Star* is a perfect boat for light conditions, but I think it is a bad boat for all-round sailing and hard weather. The *Star* upwind is hopeless in weather like it is in England and up north here, therefore I think it is really a bad boat because in strong winds it is so slow upwind and that is not fun. To be competitive even in light winds you've got to rely enormously on your sailmaker, but that's part of the game. It's a lovely feeling to sail a *Star* in light winds upwind, but downwind in light

winds it is hopeless, because there is nothing you can do and you
would like a spinnaker. In the opposite way, in strong wind upwind it is
hopeless, but downwind it is wonderful, so generally speaking it is not an
all-round boat. It is a boat for special occasions.

I like the *Dragon,* but it is too expensive to be an Olympic boat. We
cannot discuss any boat for the Olympics if it is too expensive. Then we
go to the *Soling.* It's cheaper than the *Dragon* and it keeps its value
better. It is a good boat and it's nice to sail.

When I was a boy I remember that I thought that only dinghies
should be allowed in the Olympics, because everyone could afford to
buy a dinghy and today, when I can afford to buy a keelboat, I will not
forget how I thought when I was a boy. The main reason why we still
have keelboats in the Olympics is because the people who make the
decisions as to what classes shall be Olympic are one hundred per cent
only interested in keelboats. They like keelboats because they are too
old for top dinghy racing, and they forget how they felt when they were
young people. Of course, the people who are on the committee are the
older people, because they are the people who have more time, so the
only thing I can blame them for is that they have forgotten completely
how they thought when they were young.

You can easily make a three-man dinghy where tactics would be
more important than physical condition. That could be cheap and so it
would be easy to do a three-man boat cheaply which could take a place
in the Olympics as a tactical class, instead of a keelboat. I think that
expensive boats should not be in the Olympics. We can have world
championships, we can have Gold Cups and we can have nice
regattas, but the Olympic Games are for everybody, not only for the
rich people. But, of course, the design must be a boat which gives you
pleasure.

But if there are people who are trying very hard to win an
Olympic Medal, then they are trying very hard to get their boats as fast
as possible and, therefore, they spend a lot of money—as much money
as they are allowed to spend on the boats. They buy new sails, new
masts, new boats, in the hope that they can go faster. My main idea
is that we must only choose classes that most yachting people can
afford to buy.

I can mention here that, fortunately, we have a very big range of
classes, and a sailor can race in Olympic and international boats or he
can sail in National classes or in ordinary club racing boats; so that if
someone is not prepared to put in the time to be a world-class sailor, he

204

Nordisk Presseloto

International Solings racing in the first Class World Championship near Copenhagen.

can always find somewhere where he can race against people who are doing the same amount of training, and so give him the same standard of competition. But we are talking mainly about top-racing in this story, and to be at the top in international racing there is no way round it—you have got to spend the time.

Outside assistance in racing

There is another problem we will find increasing in the coming years, and that is how much help should we allow competitors to get from outside.

It is very unsporting when one man has a lot of information and another one hasn't. For instance, in a world championship, because a country wants to get a good placing, let us say they have five power boats lying round the course and they calculate when the wind will come and they work out the tide, so that their competitor can get exact maps of the tide and information on when the wind is expected to change and so on. It costs a lot of money for that country, but it's a big advantage for that particular boat.

The I.Y.R.U. already have the rule about outside assistance, but what they will have to decide is whether to include within that ruling such things as I have mentioned.

The idea of the rules should be that all competitors can get the same information. Rule 59 says that, "a yacht shall neither receive outside assistance nor use any gear other than that on board when her preparatory signal is made." You could say that, by getting signals from a flag on a boat, he was using outside assistance. But, on the other hand, you wouldn't say that, by watching the smoke from a chimney on shore, he was using outside assistance. It would be easy to say that nobody must have an advantage over other competitors because of information that only he can get.

If a competitor is dropped last-minute weather or tide information from the air just before the start, that is information the others can't get. I mean the same aeroplane must give the information to all, but the programme must say that all information which can help any competitor must be available for all.

In this case that we are thinking of, the information was given before the start, but in a series of races it could come under Rule 49, because a boat does not have to be racing to get a protest under this rule.

This sort of thing was allowed at the Olympic Games last time, because nobody thought of trying to stop it, but I think we ought to agree that it should not continue. I think we would all agree that fair sailing is where we all have the same chance to get information, without paying a fortune. At the Olympics we now also have power boats with spare sails and gear for their competitors.

I think that in the Olympics you should not receive help from leaving the harbour till after the race and so are not to have a following boat like we saw in Acapulco. There must only be a rule before the race and not after, because then it doesn't matter and they can be towed home afterwards.

But I don't like to make more and more laws, because I can see the sort of thing happening like it is in the *Finn* class, where the measurer has to be on the slip as the boats go away. All the boats have to be collected in the same place, and you can't have people launching from different harbours round the bay, because the measurer must see all the boats go afloat and check all the gear and make sure that they come back with the same gear. It is very hard for a measurer to have to do this.

The measurers can sometimes make more problems than they solve. There was the case of Kariofillis of Greece, who won a race in the Olympics, but he was disqualified, not because the other competitors protested, but only because the measurer did not know much about *Finn* sailing. He should never have been disqualified and so there should be a rule that nobody can be disqualified without a protest from other competitors, then we can avoid that sort of unfair situation. The other competitors know what is important and what is not important, but the measurer, generally speaking, doesn't know.

In the Olympic Games of '60, especially in the *Dragon* class, there were so many protests that honestly the results in this series came from the protest table. But I must say that it is stupid of people to have too much temperament which makes them do crazy things and risk being disqualified. For instance, I remember that one boat disqualified another boat two or three minutes before the start, for misleading and baulking. When we get to that stage then it is not fun any more because, during the two or three minutes before the start, we all do what we can to avoid any collisions. There was a protest only because it was too important to these competitors that they should win.

It is not necessary to put in a protest in the case of a genuine accident. That's my feeling and I myself never protest unless some other boat is too rude or makes the same mistake twice, or a boat really breaks the rules on purpose. But most boats break the rules because the skippers are nervous or they calculate wrongly—an error of judgment and you can yourself normally see the reason for the breaking of the rule. So I would say that nobody should protest unless the other has done something deliberately.

Protests can spoil the comradeship. If I make a mistake I prefer to leave the course.

I remember once in the *5·5-metres* that Sundelin, who won the Gold Medal in Acapulco, and I started too early and neither of us noticed. The committee called us in after the race and said they were sorry that they had to disqualify us because we had started too early. Then I said, "Why are you so sorry? We had a lovely race and who was first or who was second or who was disqualified doesn't seem to us important at all because we didn't know we were over too early". If we knew we had been too early, of course we would have started again because it would not have been fair on the others.

I like the new rule that says you can go round again after you touch a mark, because so often we have missed a good competitor because he had bad luck. It is more of a shame for his friends who have lost a competitor and quite often it has happened for one or two boats who are fighting alone. But in the new rules if one touches a mark it will only be a good laugh. He had to round once more!

It is a shame when sometimes people become not very good friends after a protest because a protest should only be an interesting discussion as to how the rules are. In Acapulco there was a particularly angry discussion on how to interpret the rules and it should not have been necessary. Therefore, I would advise anyone if there is any protest against him just to take it as it is written in the rules and not to think it's something personal against him. If you or I have to protest against anyone, tell him to let us take it as a friendly discussion about the rules. When you protest against anyone the rules say you have to tell him that you are protesting, so at the same time you can say, ''I am only protesting to clarify the rules and the situation. It is nothing personal so I hope you will take it just as a friendly discussion''.

Of course, in most protests, probably nearly all, there is an argument on the facts of the situation because people get different pictures of what has happened. In a lot of cases they argue that the other is lying but it is not always so. Some people are clearer than others when they explain a situation but maybe they are guessing how the situation really was and they are sometimes guessing wrong because they hope it happened like they say it did. Then the other man thinks

that he is lying but maybe he is not really lying so we ought not to be too critical of each other when explaining a situation. They have got to try to remember and always keep in the back of their minds that it is so difficult to remember an exact situation when you are not expecting it is going to happen. You can't remember the exact position of the boats.

Sometimes the jury makes problems by not understanding the rules of the sea. For instance, let us take a practical example; in the rule when you have to tack for an obstruction, you can ask for water from a windward boat, and in dinghy sailing the time from asking for water to the tack is very short in a big dinghy fleet so you merely call and tack at the same time. You can't do this when the boats become bigger and bigger and there are less and less boats on the course. There the windward boat can ask for more time to tack. The main thing is that when there are, let us say one hundred dinghies, everything happens so fast that a boat on port must expect all the time to meet a starboard boat and so he has to be more alert and this is the unwritten law amongst the dinghy sailors. Therefore, if there is a protest case it will be wrong of the jury to say that you may not ask for water and tack at the same time. The jury can't say that when it is like that in practice. It is an unwritten law in practice and this law is stronger than the written law in the rule book.

It is the same in life where a case is decided in the High Court and

208

The jury must
be made up
of sailors

this case is stronger than the written law. It must be the same that how we actually sail and how we actually interpret the rules is the strongest and must be the strongest. Therefore, in important meetings it is important to have experienced yachting people on rule committees.

I had a start in the *5-0-5* World Championship in La Baule that I will never forget. We had the tide against us and we were about 60 or 70 boats and there was a big advantage at the port end of the line. Because of the tide we went right up to the wrong side of the line ready to be planing down to the port end mark. I remember the Committee boat was at the port end and I planed down and tacked and crossed the line on the gun and already at that time I was about six or seven boatlengths from the nearest boat. Because of this the other boats all thought I started too early and they couldn't understand it but, of course, the Committee boat could see that it was perfectly O.K. How could I see that and nobody else? I don't understand it, but it was like that.

In Denmark in 1948 no-one knew that yachting was a popular sport and people said to me, "You are rowing very well!" And in '52 after the Olympics they said, "Oh, You are sailing!" In '56 they, at last, knew what sailing was, and today you won't find anyone who doesn't know what yachting is. Maybe it was the same in other parts of the world but it was certainly like that here. I felt it very strongly. These four Gold Medals in our small country of Denmark have been pushing yachting as a sport for more people than before and after the first Gold Medal in Torquay a completely new generation started racing in Denmark. Everyone wanted to sail dinghies instead of keelboats and so the dinghy classes were really growing after '48. It is the same if you have bicycling on television and 6-day races, all the boys are then cycling afterwards.

But though sailing increased it wasn't the case in the *Finn* class in Denmark. After Torquay they had a big discussion what boat they should sail and it was decided to start the *Snipe* in Denmark. Then when the *Finn* came along and I again won in the *Finn* this time, the class still didn't increase. People were not interested in the Olympics. They were only interested in sailing. The publicity increased sailing. It didn't increase Olympic sailing. When we got the *Finn* some people hoped that they had a chance but they were so far from me in handling and speed and everything that they had no chance at all.

The Press nowadays are very active in yachting and when they write on racing it is mainly because of the Olympics. There are a lot of journalists who know nothing about yachting who write about the

209

yachtsman, as they do in other sports, as if we were boys and girls of 18 years old taking part in a sports game and this is really wrong. They always give a wrong picture of yachtsmen and therefore the Press cause a lot of problems because yachtsmen are completely in another category to people in other sports. Yachtsmen are, may I say, generally speaking more intelligent than most people in other sports and they are often older people with a lot of experience of life. People take part in yacht racing because they enjoy the sport and they are not thinking of being famous as they do in many other sports. Yachting people are not so interested in seeing their names in the Press so much. Therefore, the Press in the Olympic Games spoil the good atmosphere in yachting.

The Olympic spirit

The atmosphere in the Olympic Games in '48 and today is quite different because in 1948 none of us really knew each other. So there were a lot of problems which never would happen today in the Olympics because, when the helmsmen know each other, they don't protest when some small mistake is made in a race. They know that their friends don't break the rules on purpose.

In another way the atmosphere is sharper today; the Press is more active than in '48 and yachting itself has grown enormously so that competing in the Olympic Games today is really more interesting because more people talk about it.

The atmosphere from Games to Games is quite different; in Torquay we were all in the same harbour and that was a good way of starting knowing each other, but we lived in different hotels which was bad. The same happened in Helsinki, but there it was even worse because some countries were in one club and other countries in another. We were split into three different places. In Melbourne we nearly all lived in the Olympic Village and, therefore, we didn't see each other there and we were based in four or five different clubs along the bay. But the atmosphere there was rather special, I think, because the Australian people took an interest in us in such a way that we felt happy and welcome and like members of the family. Because we had only one class in each club it maybe improved the friendship among the competitors in each class.

In Naples we lived in different hotels and were in three clubs and it was something like Helsinki in feeling and atmosphere. I must say the best atmosphere among the competitors was in Tokyo where we all, except the Americans, were living at the same hotel. So we ate breakfast and dinner all together and also we were all in the same club house in the same harbour. It couldn't have been better and the man responsible

Paul enjoys a joke with King Paul of the Hellenes, Princess Irene and Queen Frederika during his visit there at their invitation.

D. Patridis

was Mr. Ozawa and all the competitors complimented him on this fantastic arrangement.

The Mexican organisation was nearly the same as in Japan and I must say they succeeded. They only had one big problem which was that the yachtsmen were not allowed to live together with their wives and there was no way to break that rule. But the atmosphere in Mexico was exactly the same as in Tokyo.

I would like to tell here a little story about the Norwegian King and Crown Prince because I think it is nice that in the sport of yachting we can make friends and none of us is thinking what we are, or what we do outside yachting. It was in London during the time of the IYRU Annual Meetings, and one day, when there was no meeting, I met King Olaf and Crown Prince Harald at Captain Watts' shop. We had competed against one another in Copenhagen in the World Championship the year before, and so we knew each other from there, and we stood and talked for half-an-hour about everything to do with yachting. I like to tell this, because it is not usual that you can stay and talk with a King and Crown Prince for half-an-hour in a shop, but that proves how yachting can make us all the same people. We have the same interests and, therefore, none of us is thinking what we are.

After the Olympics of '60 Aage Birch and Italian *Dragon* sailor, Sergio Sorrentino from Trieste in Italy, and myself were invited by the Greek Royal Family to sail some friendly races with them. They had five *Dragons* and the idea was that they would like us to crew them and in that way teach them a little. We had a splendid week or ten days where we were not only sailing but the Royal Family showed us Athens and the country around and they were very kind to us.

I was sailing with King Paul who was a very charming quiet man and I think he couldn't have had a worse person than me because still at that time I had my awful temperament. I remember in one race I told King Paul to tack and he did not understand me properly and was too late. So by the time he finally tacked he then shouldn't tack because the wind had shifted back. I said, "Go back!" and the result was that in the light wind we were stopped head to wind. So I took the tiller and pushed it hard to get us back to the right tack and it looked from outside very amusing. I remember King Paul said, "If you just tell me what I have to do I will do it". He really had a sense of humour. I remember in light wind we didn't do so well but in strong winds he was tremendously good on the tiller. He was an ex-*Star-boat* skipper and I must say that for his age he was really sailing very well.

I have made a lot of friends amongst the yachtsmen and I would like to say a little about some of them. Erik Johansen has been talked about already in the book. Richard Creagh-Osborne, I have known since 1956 and he has helped me with all my books except the first, 'Guld til Danmark" and also helped start the bailer business.

I would like to talk now about Henri Leten who was the first President of the *Finn* Association. I met him for the first time when I

212

Other sailing
friends

Richard Creagh-Osborne.

took part in the Zeebrugge Spring Races which are always on the
week-end nearest the 1st May. Because of his initiative the
Zeebrugge races became very famous. The *Finn* boys from France,
Netherlands, Belgium, England, Scandinavia, Germany and Italy, met
each other in Zeebrugge and Henri Leten organized it in such a charming
way that we all loved to go back every year.

The water in Zeebrugge is dirty, with big tides and strong
currents, but interesting because it was always different and we had a
lot of fun. We capsized and some of us were standing in oily mud and
then we had two months' work after that to clean the boats, but we had
a lot of laughs because always something happened in Zeebrugge.
Henri Leten worked very hard for the young people in Belgium. He
started the *Cadet* class and was very enthusiastic about helping the
young people and making yachting more popular. Today he is a
member of the IYRU Small Boat Committee in London and it is very
nice to see how such a man sticks to this business of helping yachting.
He has an ocean racer himself and is very active but his main interest
is to make other people happy.

The year after the accident on the autobahn we came to Zeebrugge
again and he gave me a model of a fishing boat. It was 80 cm long and
very accurately made and he gave it to me to thank me for coming
back every year. I liked the ship so much, not because it is an accurate

213

model of an Ostend fishing boat but because I know that Henri loves model ships of all kinds and especially the old ones, and it is very characteristic of Henri to give away a thing he loves best.

Helmar Petersen was Paul's reserve at Helsinki in 1952, but later emigrated to New Zealand and won the Flying Dutchman Gold Medal at Tokyo.

Helmar Petersen from New Zealand was originally a Dane. He was my spare man in '52 in Helsinki and after the Games he emigrated to New Zealand and became a New Zealand citizen. He started by sailing *Finns* and then went over to *Flying Dutchman* and became selected for New Zealand for the Tokyo Olympic Games where he won the Gold Medal. We have always been friends since we were training together in 1951/52.

We were both house-builders and we both went to the same school of architecture and in the autumn of 1951 we both had one month's holiday and so we spent that month sailing every day for between 5 and 8 hours. We became so equal that if he started first he won and if I started first I won. In 1952 Helmar became a soldier so that he didn't have as much time as I had to continue training. So when we came to the selection races I came first and he was second.

214

Colin Ryrie from Sydney I met first in '56 when he represented Australia in the Olympic Games in the *Finn* class and I remember the first time I really got in contact with Colin was on a day that it was blowing very hard. I went out with a new cotton sail and came in after two hours sailing and Colin said, "Isn't it wrong to go out with a completely new sail in such a strong wind—don't you spoil the shape?" and so I said, "One of the most important things in the *Finn* is to have a long leach and my leach is 4" longer than yours because you have not been out sailing", "Is that really true?" he said. "Yes, I will show you". So we put our sails on top of each other and the curve on my sail's leach was a little smaller but the length of the leach was 4" longer. So Colin went out immediately though there was a risk of capsizing in such a strong wind and that would have been worse because then the cotton sail would have been smaller and flatter.

After that I had a very close connection with Colin and one year he got the idea of making some sails in Sydney together with me. So today he has a nice sail loft called "Elvström Sails" in Sydney and this came from the old friendship we got in '56. Colin took part later in the Olympic Games in Tokyo, also in *Finns*, where he got a very good place.

Jack Knights.

A chap like Jack Knights everybody in the whole world knows because of his articles. I met Jack for the first time in Kiel Week in '54, before the English had their trials for the Olympic Games in Melbourne. I found him a very good hard wind sailor at the time and respected him even then as a very hard competitor.

Later I met Jack as spare man for Richard Creagh-Osborne in Melbourne and year after year I met him again in all sorts of classes. Jack has won a lot of championships but he has never concentrated hard enough in one class to be able to win the biggest Olympic or world championships. Jack has a very good character and he always says what he thinks. In my experience he thinks always about what is best for yachting and criticizes anything that makes yachting poor. I would say that he is one of the few journalists who is positive in his articles. It is very rare that he criticizes anything without proposing something better and that I think is very fine with him.

There are many, many other friends and there is only room for some to have been mentioned in the book. I cannot talk about them all here but I would like to thank them now for the nice sailing we have had together and I hope we can meet many times more.

Anne has been a wonderful wife to me and she knows that I have to go out sailing and she does nothing now to try to stop me because for three or four years I was not racing and I was the worst person you could be with. I was so angry. I was sitting with my binoculars watching races and I know that I longed to take part in a race but then I forced myself to be sitting watching. But it was very good that I forced myself not to take part.

I did two races a year but I went out tuning boats, I was sailing a lot but not racing. For instance I was once tuning a *Knaar-boat* and the owner said he couldn't get the boat going and at that time he had one of our first *Knaar* sails and I was very disappointed. So I went out with him.

From the first I found that he couldn't steer properly so we took the boat out and fixed the rudder so that it was free and he could feel the boat. Then I adjusted the mast and then I said it *must* go faster now. But he said, "Can't you steer the boat for me in an evening race", and I said, "O.K. let us try". We don't know who was second—it was light wind—so far ahead were we. Then he said, "Now I hope I can do the same". And the next Saturday and Sunday it was light winds and he won by a quarter of an hour or something like that. A quarter of an hour ahead of No. 2! So fantastic! O.K. a fortnight later all the *Knaar-boats*

216

Mr. K. Ozawa, the organiser of the yachting in the 1964 Olympic Games, talks to Paul and Anne Elvström during one of their visits to Japan, at his invitation.

had our sails. I won't say that that was racing. I took part in a race just to tune the boat.

No, I was very active but mainly I was in a power boat, my little speed boat, and I have learned more racing from watching than you could learn from sailing a boat and when I started sailing again I was a better tactician than before. Otherwise I could never do what I did in the *5·5-metre*, the *Star,* the *5-0-5* and the *Soling.* And I had not sailed a *5-0-5* for *eight years*.

I would say the main thing was that before the nervous breakdown I was instinctively doing that and that but I was not sure why I did it. When I stopped and watched races for three or four years from the power-boat I was able to work out what I should do to get the right position. You are never sure because always you need luck. For example you can say that in that situation there is the biggest chance that the wind will go back so therefore you have to go over there. If it doesn't go back, O.K. then it's bad luck, but you must calculate what the wind will do and what you must do because of the wind and the tide. You must calculate all the time.

If I should say what interests me it would be designing and testing ideas but it is so expensive that I can't afford to do much of it. I have tried many ideas and of course one or two have gone into production and have been very successful. The best was the bailer, which of course every dinghy sailor needed. Then there was the winch-block, and of course the *Trapez* dinghy in the end proved very successful after a tremendous amount of hard work.

When I came back from the 1948 Olympics and started to prepare for the next Olympics, I remember as if it was today, that I told my brother that I calculated that theoretically I could win this Gold Medal six times. I said this to him then and I could have done it if I had not had the nervous breakdown. Now I know I can never do it because I don't have the energy of a young man. I start feeling old. It is not so much feeling old in body but you change in the mind. You lose your drive for racing. When we realize that life is so short I think we all feel that it is a little more important to have enjoyment with friends.

Some years ago I had a dream that I was ill and was going to die. And in the dream I remember I said to myself, "What have you done in your life. You have been working so hard to win a Gold Medal and now you are going to die. Why have you done all this?" Because honestly, I worked hard to be in that position in a *Finn.* Often I went out sailing *Finns* and it was not fun at all to go hanging in the sea in a strong wind quite alone, and the Finn is an awful boat when you are sailing alone without competition. In light winds you enjoy sailing *Finns* and also in medium winds, but in strong winds with a choppy sea you are not moving at all. I often said to myself, "Why are you doing this? It is not

218

Paul looks a little unhappy at the helm of an offshore racer.

fun". But I did it because I was trying to be faster to get a good result on a racing course. But it is something you cannot continue doing always. I realized then that life is short and you must do what gives you pleasure.

I asked myself. Did I enjoy achieving these results? No, honestly it was a duty—I think a duty to my way of living. My mother taught me that I had to work and do things properly. It was something I had grown up with from my mother. Maybe it was a complex.

My wife Anne and my family

My first daughter came just before we started the sail loft in 1954. I had no more money. All my savings had gone into the sail loft and so Anne got nothing at that time. Honestly, it must not have been nice for her. I don't think it is nice to have married a too active man. Of course, I was too active then and so it was very difficult for Anne in those days and maybe it still is because a chap who is sailing can't be a family man. Remember, a man who has no hobby is with the family at the week-ends, and we who are sailing are always out sailing. It is an advantage that I am living so that Anne can see me sailing, but being out at work all day, come home late, start again early and sailing in the week-ends—it can't be nice.

Now I have four girls and sometimes I have been so disappointed that in winter-time they are playing with dolls and we have a ping-pong table and no one played ping-pong. It would have been nice to

219

Jens Frellsen

Niels Benzon, President of the Royal Danish Yacht Club and the man who beat Paul in Paul's first-ever race in the Oslo-dinghy *congratulates him after winning his second Star World Championship title.*

have had a boy I could play with.

I continue sailing because I like it. No one would do his business in the week-end if he didn't like it. My business is sailmaking. I started it because I liked it and I still like it, and it is wonderful to produce something you like. It's a short life and you should only do what you like.

Obviously I must sail at week-ends if I am to get experience because that is when everybody else is sailing, but I must honestly say

Now I can
sail for fun!

that when I am sailing I am one hundred per cent sailing because I like to sail that boat and I like to try new things. It has nothing to do with the business—just because it's fun. Otherwise I could take the powerboat and watch the sails we had made from that and find out in that way. No! I go out sailing because it is fun.

If I could afford it I would like to have a big boat so that I could have the family with me because there are so many nice places in Scandinavia that we could go to. But at the same time I like racing and you can't do both, so I hope in my old age, the charm for me will be cruising.

I don't want to force the girls to come sailing if they don't want to. They are sailing at school but they are not enthusiastic at all. I think they sail because they have to do something. They don't love it.

I think that whatever happens I feel I have to be on the water. It is something which I can't avoid doing. I remember the Sunday mornings when I went out in my rowing boat as a boy—just going out and floating on the water—it was happiness itself. It's something that most women don't understand at all. There are some that understand it, but very few, and you can't explain it to them. But I must say that not all boats, I mean not all things which float, give me pleasure. There must be some liveliness in what I am floating on.

221